THE MOMENT
UNDER
THE MOMENT

THE MOMENT
UNDER
THE MOMENT

Stories, a Libretto, Essays and Sketches

Russell Hoban

JONATHAN CAPE
LONDON

First published 1992
© Russell Hoban 1992
Jonathan Cape, 20 Vauxhall Bridge Road, London SW1V 2SA

The following first appeared: 'My night with Léonie' in
Sphinx; 'Schwartz' in *Encounter*; 'Dream Woman' in *Fiction
Magazine*; 'Dark Oliver' in the *Observer Magazine*; 'The
Ghost Horse of Genghis Khan' in the *Listener*; 'Blighter's
Rock' in *The Pauline*; 'The Bear in Max Ernst's Bedroom' in
Brick; 'The Man with the Dagger', 'Pan Lives', 'Fragments of a
Lament for Thelonious Monk', 'Footplacers, London
Transport Owls, Wincer-Boise' and 'Mnemosyne, Teen Taals,
and Tottenham Court Road' in *Granta*. 'Household Tales'
was first published as an introduction to *Household Tales* by
the Brothers Grimm (Picador, 1977); 'With a Choked Cry' was
first published in the catalogue, *Box of Delights*, for a
children's book illustration exhibition at Newport Museum
and Art Gallery, Newport, Gwent; and 'Portknockie' was first
published in *Places*, ed. Ronald Blythe (OUP, 1981).

Russell Hoban has asserted his right under the Copyright,
Designs and Patents Act 1988 to be identified as the author of
this work

Excerpt from *Little Gidding* by T. S. Eliot,
reprinted by kind permission of Faber & Faber Ltd.

A CIP catalogue record for this book is available from the
British Library

ISBN 0–224–03314–X

Printed in Great Britain by
Mackays of Chatham PLC, Chatham, Kent

For my sisters,
Tana and Freeda

Contents

Foreword

Reality is ungraspable. For convenience we use a limited-reality consensus in which work can be done, transport arranged, and essential services provided. The *real* reality is something else – only the strangeness of it can be taken in and that's what interests me: the strangeness of human consciousness; the strangeness of life and death; the strangeness of what the living and the dead are to one another; and the strangeness of ideas – Orpheus and Eurydice for example, Miranda and Caliban, King Kong and Fay Wray – that seem to have been with us from long before the stories of them happened.

The real reality, the flickering of seen and unseen actualities, the moment under the moment, can't be put into words; the most that a writer can do – and this is only rarely achieved – is to write in such a way that the reader finds himself in a place where the unwordable happens off the page. Most of the time it doesn't happen but trying for it is part of being the hunting-and-finding animal one is. This process is what I care about and what I write is as much process as product.

Reading over these pages has been a humbling experience. I was shocked to find that the word *tawny* appeared fifteen times and *tawniness* twice; with a tremendous effort I managed to kill all but four of the tawnies. I feel all right about the stories but some of the essays are wetter in places than I'd like. But as I've already said, process is what I care about and this is it.

STORIES

The Man with the Dagger

There is a short story by Jorge Luis Borges called 'The South'. It is a story full of sharpness, having in it a lance, a sword, the edge of a door, two knives, the strangeness of life and the familiarity of death.

The protagonist of the story is Juan Dahlmann, secretary to a municipal library in Buenos Aires in 1939. His paternal grandfather, a German immigrant, was a minister in the Evangelical Church. His maternal grandfather was 'that Francisco Flores, of the Second Line-Infantry Division, who had died on the frontier of Buenos Aires, run through with a lance by Indians from Catriel ... ' Dahlmann keeps the sword of Francisco Flores and his daguerreotype portrait, and has, 'at the cost of numerous small privations ... managed to save the empty shell of a ranch in the South which had belonged to the Flores family'. He has never lived on this ranch; year after year it waits for him.

Hurrying up the library stairs one day, Dahlmann strikes his head against the edge of a freshly painted door and comes away with a bloody wound. The next morning 'the savour of all things was atrociously poignant. Fever wasted him ... ' He nearly dies of septicaemia, and after a long stay in a sanatorium he leaves the city to go to his ranch for his convalescence.

On his arrival in the South he has a meal at a general store near the railway station. Three men are drinking at another table; one of them has a Chinese look. This man provokes Dahlmann by throwing breadcrumb spitballs at him, then challenges him to a knife fight. Dahlmann knows nothing of knifeplay and is unarmed but an old gaucho throws him a naked dagger which lands at his feet. 'It was as if the South had resolved that Dahlmann should accept the duel. Dahlmann bent over to pick up the dagger and felt two things. The first, that this almost instinctive act bound him to fight. The second, that the weapon, in his torpid hand, was no defence at all, but would merely serve to justify his murder.'

Dahlmann picks up the dagger and goes out into the plain to fight. 'Without hope, he was also without fear ... He felt that if he had been able to choose, then, or to dream his death, this would have been the death he would have chosen or dreamt.'

With the dagger Dahlmann has seized the critical moment that defines ... what? The right time to die? No use to attempt an analysis of Borges's intention – by the time Dahlmann picks up the dagger he is a fiction of his own making.

Now for as long as there will be print on paper, even longer – for as long as there will be one rememberer to pass this story on to another, even longer, even when all the rememberers are dead, Dahlmann, with his being vibrating between the strangeness of life and the familiarity of death, will live in this moment of unknown definition that he has seized. I wanted to talk to him.

The White Street

I thought the story would be the most likely place to look for Dahlmann, so I went there. I found it in a quiet street where the trees made little black shadows in a dazzling whiteness; it was an old rose-coloured house with iron grill windows, a brass knocker, and an arched door. Beside the door was a brass plaque; engraved on it in copperplate script: *The South*.

I knocked, and after a time I heard slow footsteps within and the thud of bolts being drawn back. The door opened slowly and in a very narrow aperture there appeared a vertical fraction of an old woman's face at the top of a blackness of clothing. Her one visible eye was black and difficult to meet.

'Good afternoon,' I said (my watch had stopped but the street was white with heat and light and the sun seemed almost directly overhead). 'Is Señor Dahlmann at home?'

'There's no one here,' she said. 'We're closed.' The aperture and her face became narrower and disappeared with a click. There was the sound of bolts thudding home; her footsteps receded. Behind me the white street shimmered in the heat; far away a dog barked. I didn't want to turn around and see that white street again; I felt myself to be a prism through which the white light would reveal its full spectrum of terror.

I stood facing the centuries-darkened door until I felt myself flickering into black-and-white, then I turned back to the street. It too was flickering in black-and-white like an old film in which nothing had yet happened.

There was a boy flickering in front of me. His head was bent so that his straw sombrero concealed his face, his hands were behind his back. I didn't notice his feet.

'Where's Dahlmann?' I said.

'New in town?'

'Yes.'

'Do they have discretion where you come from?'

'Some do.'

'But not you.'

'I'm a writer, I need to know things.'

'What you need is not to be in too much of a hurry. I'll take you to the hotel.'

His manner was that of one who has seen everything. 'I bet the stories you could tell would make a hell of a book,' I said, 'if only you knew how to get them down on paper.'

He shrugged. 'Not everything needs to be written down.'

We walked without speaking past many churches and past many squares with fountains. Everything continued black-and-white, the streets gradually filling with voices and footsteps and people. Eventually there appeared, not in the most expensive part of town, a small hotel with its name in unlit neon tubing: HOTEL DEATH. On its glass doors were the emblems of American Express, Diners' Club, and Visa. Opposite was a square with a fountain; on the far side of the square was a church.

'I'll see you later,' said the boy, and wasn't there any more.

Hotel Death

'What can I do for you?' said the skeleton at the desk. He was wearing a garish print shirt outside his trousers, he had a bottle of whisky and a glass and he was smoking an inexpensive cigar. The black-and-white was holding steady. A slowly turning fan in the ceiling stirred the grey shadows and the drifting dust-motes in the lobby.

'Have you got a Señor Dahlmann registered here?' I said.

He blew out a big cloud of inexpensive-smelling smoke. It came out of his mouth in the usual way. 'No.'

'You haven't looked.'

'I don't need to.' He poured himself a whisky and lifted his glass. 'Here's looking at you.'

I looked into the hollows where his eyes would have been; the shadows were not unfriendly. The whisky didn't run out of the back of his jaw, it just disappeared. He noticed my staring.

'It didn't bother you that I can talk without a tongue but you draw the line at drinking without a throat, is that it?'

'Not at all,' I lied.

'You want to check in?'

6

'No.'

'You look pretty old. Why not do it now and beat the rush? We got TV in every room and if you get lonesome I can send somebody around.'

'Skeleton whores?'

'Don't knock it till you've tried it.'

'Later,' I said. 'I've still got things to do.'

'Like what?'

'Like finding Dahlmann.'

'Are you sure you want to?'

'That's what I came here for.'

'Are you sure?'

'Look, let's not turn this into a philosophical exercise. I'll see you later.'

'You know it.'

I went outside and stood by the doors and stared at the flickering black-and-white of the church and the square and the fountain and the dusty street through which passed mules and ox-carts and dark people with sandalled feet and white cotton clothing. There was a smell of faeces and rotting fruit; there were the tolling of a bell and the buzzing of flies. From an upstairs window came the sound of a guitar.

There was a little whiff of lemony fragrance. 'Hi,' said a soft voice next to me. I turned and saw a really stunning skeleton with just the faintest touch of grey on her cheek-bones; I recognised it as blusher. No eye shadow, her eyes were nothing but shadows. She was wearing a black poncho, a shiny black Rudolph Valentino hat with a flat top and a broad brim, and black boots. She was shapely in a way that made flesh seem vulgar.

'Why the blusher?' I said.

'I've seen things. Why are you looking for Dahlmann?'

'I think he may have something to tell me.'

'Perhaps I too have something to tell you.'

Together we walked off into the sunlight that would

7

have made a blackness before my eyes if we had been in colour.

Noir's Room

I thought she would rattle but she didn't. What happened was that after the first few moments she stopped being a skeleton for me and simply became who she was, clean and elegant and more naked than I should have thought possible. With her lemony fragrance and that improbable blush on her cheekbones she was utterly girlish in my arms while there echoed in my mind an ancient scream of desolation and all sweetness gone, gone, gone with her clean white feet running and her black poncho flapping down endless corridors of neverness.

'What's your name?' I said.

'Noir.'

'How much do I owe you, Noir?'

'Nothing, I'm not working now.'

'Why aren't you working now?'

'Sometimes I make love for money and sometimes I do it for me. This one was for me.'

'How come?'

'You ever do it with a skeleton before?'

'No.'

'I wanted your skeleton cherry,' she said, and kissed me. The room was a subtle composition of grey and black shadows with lines of brilliant white between the slats of the blinds. Through the front window came the sounds of a street market. On a table there were white lemons in a basket, there was a bottle of gin. I could feel colour impending but I held on to the black-and-white. Across the patio someone with a guitar was playing and singing a tango. The shadowy guitar and the quiet husky male voice made the gin seem miraculous.

'What do the words mean?' I asked her.

She listened for a moment, then she whispered in my ear:

8

'Such a little, such a little, such a little
difference, my heart –
such a little difference between the one
and the other.'

'Is it really such a little difference?' I said.

'Listen,' she said with her mouth still close to my ear,
'I'll sing you a verse of my own:

You were with me, with me, with me, my heart –
you were naked in my arms, to you
I gave my naked self, my onlyness.
Was it less than you've had from others?'

I kissed her delicate ivory face. Her mouth was sweet.

'Don't go looking for Dahlmann,' she said. 'What can
he tell you that I can't?'

'I don't know. I don't even know what I'm going to ask
him.' I got out of bed and put my clothes on. I didn't look
back at her as I opened the door and went out.

'It could have been good,' she said.

Sidekick

Again I was hearing the buzzing of flies in a street that
smelled of faeces and rotting fruit. Here also there were
a square and a fountain and a church; the market stalls
clustered under awnings along the near side of the square.
The flickering seemed a little less steady than before.

There was a skeleton boy with his hat over his eyes, he
was sitting on the ground leaning against the house I'd just
come out of. He pushed the hat back and looked up at me
as if expecting something.

'What is it?' I said.

'Don't you recognise me?'

'No.'

'I'm the kid that took you to the hotel.'

9

'Funny, I never noticed you were so bony. This place is full of regular people; why am I always talking to skeletons?'

'Maybe you speak our language.'

'Why is that? Am I dead?'

'What a question! You don't ask questions like that around here, it isn't that kind of a place, there's nothing that simple.'

'All right, then, I'll ask you something else: what's your interest in me? Why did you take me to that hotel and why have you been waiting for me here?'

'What's the matter with you? Don't you go to the movies? I'm the little clever street kid who helps you out; I'm your sidekick, I'm the only one on your side.'

'What's your name?'

'Whitey.'

'What about Noir? Isn't she on my side?'

'Shit. Women!'

'Well, is she or isn't she?'

'She's my sister but she hasn't got much sense and she gets mixed up with all kinds of people.'

'Like me.'

'And others.'

'What others?'

'All kinds. You see that big guy in the rumpled white suit down at the end of the square?'

I looked. The man was over six and a half feet tall, weighed about three hundred pounds, and appeared to be the standard sort of henchman or subordinate villain one sees in films. He had nothing of a Chinese look about him and he was not entirely unfamiliar to me but I seemed not to remember who he was. 'Who's he?' I said.

'Don't you know?'

'Why should I know?'

'Because this is that kind of a place, some of us are skeletons and some are extras but anybody else with any real action in the story is somebody you know.'

'Maybe I'll know him later but I don't know him now. You say he's one of the people Noir's mixed up with?'

'I'm not sure.'

'Never mind him for now. What about Dahlmann?'

'What?'

'Do you know where he is?'

'I don't exactly know where he is but I think I know when you can find him.'

'When will that be?'

'Later. Have another look around the square.'

I had another look. There was a second big man more or less the same as the first one. Now I seemed to be remembering these men from times when they were less big and I was much younger: the first one would be . . . John? John Something. Tum-tee-tum. DeGrassi? Bonanno? 'We'll settle this after school down by the boathouse,' he'd said. I'd preferred not to. Long, long ago. Some things you walk away from and they walk after you. I'd fought Joe Higgins and I'd lost but that had never bothered me. The second one, was he Sergeant Somebody from my army days whose offer to take off his stripes and step outside I'd declined? Matson? Mason?

' . . . around the square,' said Whitey.

'What did you say?'

'Have another look around the square.'

There was a third big man in a rumpled white suit. He was from no more than fifteen years ago, this one. I'd never known his name; he'd been a stranger in a bar, another of my backdowns. 'What's happening?' I said. 'Is this the day when all my cowardice falls due?'

'What can I tell you? Every day has in it all your days. The past is something that sticks to your shoes like cowshit. If Yesterday had kept his pants on Tomorrow wouldn't have a big belly. Run is a good dog but Fight is a better one.'

'O God, skeleton aphorisms.'

'When I first saw you, you were knocking at the door

of *The South*. Why were you knocking at that door?'

'I wanted to ask Dahlmann what happened when he picked up the knife.'

'Why?'

'It's something I've thought about for a long time.'

'Why?'

'Various reasons.'

'Maybe because there were so many knives you didn't pick up?'

'What are you, the skeleton of Sigmund Freud as a boy?'

'No, I'm your sidekick. I'm the clever little street kid who helps you and I'd like to know how many big guys in rumpled white suits we're talking about. How many are there altogether?'

'More than one would like, certainly.'

'Then let's get out of here before more of them turn up. One thing . . . '

'What?'

'What you're doing now, keep it going as long as you can until you're ready for the other.'

'You mean keep the black-and . . . '

'Discretion.'

'And the other?'

'Is what you think it is.'

It was night. Flickering steadily I moved the slats of the blind apart and looked down into a deserted black-and-white square with a ruined fountain. 'I'm tired of running,' I said.

'I love it when you talk discreet,' said Whitey.

Night Run

We were in the deserted square. The streetlamps offered only a feeble and hopeless glimmer that seemed continually to be swallowed up in obscurity. Dim lights punctuated the darkness at odd intervals. Whitey and I stood listening to footsteps that never receded into the distance quite as they should have done.

'Let's get ourselves a car,' he said. We crossed to the far side of the square and he slipped along silently trying doors until an infirm pickup truck opened for us. We climbed in, Whitey was busy with his hands under the dashboard, there were sparks, the motor started with a roar and we were off.

'Turn on the headlamps for Christ's sake,' I said.

'It's better that you don't see too much, you'll lose your nerve.' Rattling and roaring we disappeared into the obscurity that had swallowed up the feeble glimmer of the streetlamps.

John Kobassa & Co.

There was a van blocking the road. In the beams of its headlamps I saw Noir struggling in the grip of one of the big men in rumpled white suits. Whitey braked hard and we jolted to a stop in a cloud of dust. The other two big men were there as well.

'I knew this was going to happen,' I said.

'What did you expect?' said Whitey. 'Cucumber sandwiches?'

'I guess not. But really . . . '

'What?'

'What can they do to her? She's already a skeleton.'

'What a gringo you are.'

'What do you mean by that?'

'Honour is nothing to you, eh? Do you want to watch all three of them having my sister here in front of you? Is that the sort of thing you like?'

'No, I shouldn't like that at all.'

'"No, I shouldn't like that at all,"' he mocked. 'What are you going to do about it? Have you got balls or are you a miserable capon?'

'Aren't you going to help? She's your sister.'

'I'll do sidekick things, like stand on the bonnet and hit them with the starting handle if they get close enough.'

I got out of the truck. Now I remembered them clearly: John Kobassa; Sergeant Moxon; Nameless Stranger.

'You remember us, do you?' said John. He was the one holding Noir.

'Don't worry about me,' Noir said. 'There's nothing they can do to me that hasn't been done before.'

'They're not going to do anything to you,' I said. 'It's me they want. Let her go,' I said to John. 'Here I am.'

'It's about time,' said John.

'Hello, chicken,' said Sergeant Moxon. 'I've been waiting for you for forty-three years.'

'I'm here now. How come all of you are so much bigger than I remember and nobody's old except me?'

'That's how it goes when you put things off too long,' said Nameless Stranger. 'Now if you're ready, we'll do what we didn't do that other time.'

So we did it. When I came to, the pickup's headlamps were on, the three big men and the van had gone, and Noir was kissing me. I'd been very wise to keep it black-and-white; if it had been full colour they might well have finished me off altogether. As it was, I doubted that my injuries were any worse than if I'd been run over by a medium-sized car: seven or eight of my ribs were broken along with one or two limbs, my head, and my dentures; also there seemed to be a fair amount of bleeding both external and internal. All in all I thought it best not to try anything too active for a while so I stayed where I was and looked at Noir out of my one working eye.

'How are you?' she said.

'Terrific,' I mumbled toothlessly. 'If I'd known how good I was going to feel afterwards I'd have looked them up sooner.' It was then that I noticed that the blusher on her cheekbones was pink and not grey and things weren't flickering any more. 'Where's Whitey?' I said.

'Here I am.' He was climbing down from the top of the pickup.

'Did you stand on the bonnet and hit them with the starting handle?'

'Nobody came close enough.'

'Can we find Dahlmann now?'

'You don't have to find me,' said a new voice. 'I've found you.'

'You're Dahlmann?'

'I'm Dahlmann.'

Without ever having seen a photograph of Borges that indicated his height I'd always thought of him as a short man and I'd assumed that Dahlmann would be short as well, so I was surprised to see that he was a tall thin man of forty or so, wearing a rumpled white suit but nonetheless elegant and soldierly in his bearing. His face was long and narrow, with the watchful eyes and cultivated blankness of a man of action; his hair was very black and he had just such a daguerreotypical beard as Francisco Flores must have worn.

'Why were you looking for me?' he said in a perfectly flat and uninflected voice.

Had I expected friendliness? I couldn't remember. I tried to scramble to my feet but one of my legs gave way. Noir came to me and effortlessly lifted me up, then drew back and stood watching me intently. Before the unforeseen actuality of Dahlmann I tried to be as dignified as possible. I no longer wanted to speak the words that I had planned to say but I spoke them as if damned and preordained to do so: 'I wanted to talk to you about what you did, I wanted to know what happened and how it was when you took the dagger in your hand and went out into the plain.' What I said sounded wet and stupid and it was a lie: I no longer wanted to know what had happened and how it had been; I just wanted to go home. I looked at Noir and she blew me a kiss.

'You mean this dagger?' he said. He threw it into the

15

air, the blade flashed in the light of the headlamps as it went end over end and the dagger returned haft-first to his hand. With his face still blank he said, 'What do you think happened?'

'I think you were killed.'

'That's your opinion, is it?'

'Yes.'

'Would you care to back that opinion?'

'How do you mean?'

'Would you like to try me?'

Inwardly I sighed but I said nothing aloud. It was night, the darkness was full of the many and mysterious colours of black. In the light of the headlamps there seemed to be a genuine blush on Noir's painted cheekbones; the shadowy hollows of her eyes sparkled with tenderness. It was night, it was dark, but in my mind a vast and tawny plain opened before me under the sun of the South as Whitey threw me a long knife that made a small hiss as it stuck into the ground at my feet.

My Night with Léonie

'What time do you get off work?' I said to her.

'Are you crazy?' she said. 'I'm a sphinx.' Her voice! Like the sea but also like honey – the wideness and the ancientness of it, the sweetness. I trembled all over.

'I can see that you're a sphinx. I asked you when you get off work.'

'We have not been introduced.' Her lips barely moved when she spoke. Her accent was enchanting; her English was perfect but it came out as if from a phrase book while she crouched immobile with naked breasts.

This was my first time in Paris. I'd have thought a French sphinx would be freer in her behaviour; her regard for convention excited and inflamed me. 'How can one introduce what is already there,' I said, 'what is already known, what has been presented from antiquity, from before antiquity even? Always you have been who you are and I have been who I am. Always what is between us has been between us.' I wanted to say simpler things, better things, but those were the words that came stilting out of my mouth.

'As you see,' she said, 'I am made of stone.'

'You are made of yourself, you are made of the magical power of your sexuality and your wisdom that is before words, before thought. You are made of the desire and the longing that you have inspired in me.'

'I'm a virgin,' she said.

'One begins where one begins,' I declared. Passers-by moved on discreetly without stopping to listen to our conversation. I believed her when she said that she was a virgin; she looked like a young person careful of her reputation. I had no idea when she might have been installed there on the south terrace of the Jardin des Tuileries at the corner of the Avenue du Général Lemonnier but I didn't suppose she was any more than two or three hundred years old. Her face was more modern than neo-classical: a plump little chin; a small, closed, unsmiling mouth; blank eyes staring straight ahead. Either a beauty mark or some birdshit high on her left cheek. Not a lovely face nor an inviting one but so erotic in its utter propriety. To see that mouth open for a kiss, to feel the bite of those presumably small and regular teeth! Her ears, behind which fell the stone stripes of her Egyptian headdress, were surprisingly large. Was it possible, I wondered, that she'd been listening all this time for someone to say what she wanted to hear. Her breasts were magnificent. Ordinarily I'm a bottom and leg man but her breasts were perfect and commanding, defiant of time and history in their ardour, their innocence, their authority. Each one was bigger than my head but these are technicalities; love conquers all. Her haunches seemed small and repressed but were provocative because of that. Her motionless tail seemed to twitch.

'I appreciate your sincerity and your conviction,' she said. 'Nothing like this has happened to me before but I am open to what life offers. If what you desire is possible then you will know when to come for me and what to say. Now you must go so that I can compose myself to be photographed by the seven Japanese gentlemen waiting patiently behind you.'

I recognised the seven Japanese as guests at the hotel where I was staying. I had seen them at breakfast and I had seen them after breakfast busy with their cameras at Saint-Germain l'Auxerrois opposite. Their greedy lenses made me anxious: I was afraid they would suck out the souls of all the buildings and places and leave only emptiness for me. The seven nodded and smiled and I nodded and smiled back.

My mind was bursting with her words as I walked away: 'If what you desire is actually possible then you will know when to come for me and what to say.' Behind her lay the unseen desert, the hot and dry waiting for the cool and wet. I was certain that what I wanted was possible because I couldn't believe myself to be so out of touch with reality as to attempt the impossible. On the other hand I wasn't sure just what it was that I wanted. Or perhaps I should say that I knew what but not precisely what kind of what. The whatness of the what was what I was uncertain of.

Her face now came to me more clearly than when I'd been standing in front of her. It was the face of any self-respecting young person pressed into service as a sphinx: not the face of anyone special but the more special because of that, the more universal. 'Yes,' I said aloud as I passed three stout German women standing by a coach and consulting their maps, 'you are the sphinx in every woman, that is your triumph and your specialness. I have slept with a number of women and I have lived with several but I have never found the right way to be with a woman, never found how to give what was in me to give. I know that to make love with you would be a kind of alchemy in which the dull and leaden self of me would be transmuted to the gold required by you.'

'*Quatsch*,' said one of the women.

'Not quatsch,' I said. 'Alchemy.'

The stone of my lion-woman had been cool and grey but in my mind she now became hot and tawny in the wide desert of me where shimmering mirages mingled with the musky colours of eastern music and the clashing of ankle bells as I hastened back to my room. The Hôtel Le Relais du Louvre is opposite the south side of Saint-Germain l'Auxerrois and my third-floor window offered a near-level *vis-à-vis* with a gargoyle with whom I had struck up an acquaintance as soon as I arrived. This was a human gargoyle, not a chimerical one. He was wearing a long-eared jester's hood and he stuck out at right angles to the cornice just below the balustrade to the right of the south porch. He was the fourth gargoyle on the right and also the last one. Four being a hermetic number I felt lucky to have arrived at the window facing him. His mouth was wide open in a perfectly dry shout as there was no rain at the moment. His mouth was so urgently, so strenuously open that I knew that if his neck were not concealed by the hood I'd have seen the veins standing out on it. This jester's expression was that of a bearer of immense tidings: the sky is falling, the end of the world is at hand – something of that magnitude. Perhaps he had tried to shout a warning on that Saint Bartholomew's Eve when in this very church the bell named *La Marie* had summoned the deaths of eight thousand Huguenots. He was sitting on the shoulders of another figure which necessarily stuck out at the same perilous right angle so that both were parallel to the ground and about ten metres above it. This second figure, which had long since lost its head, was supported by a stone bracket; on the bracket, serving as a sort of hoddy-doddy caryatid, was a squat and squarish stone woman (well past the age of lactation, I should have thought) suckling a dog. These figures had obviously demanded of the sculptor that he carve them so as to make them visible to the general public. They seemed possessed of and by a powerful sapience and I was confident of getting practical advice from the jester who appeared to be the spokesman or shoutsman for the group. There he was, rigid with open-mouthed silence in the afternoon sunlight while two pigeons walked around on him. The sunlight was singing, as foreign sunlight always does:

> This, yes this, how strange it is that this
> is this, is this, is this, is this . . .

Although there was no rain I knew that the jester could

speak if spoken to. Fixing him with my eye across the street-wide open air between us I told him what I had said to the sphinx and what she had said to me. 'What do you think?' I said.

'Go for it,' he shouted in his stone voice. He too spoke English, with a rough manner and what I took to be a medieval accent.

'Thank you for your encouragement but what I want is technical advice. When should I go back and what should I say?'

'She's by the Louvre?'

'Yes, she's at the corner of the Quai des Tuileries and the Avenue du Général Lemonnier.'

'That's First Arrondissement. In what direction is she facing?'

'East.'

'Tante Celestine,' said the jester to the stone wet-nurse: 'First Arrondissement sphinx facing east at the corner of Quai des Tuileries and Avenue du Général Lemonnier – when should our friend go back and what should he say to her?'

'He should go back when the full moon is shining on her face,' said Tante Celestine without interrupting her nourishment of the dog. 'He should say her name . . .'

'O God,' I said, 'I forgot to ask it.'

'Tante,' said the jester, 'he doesn't know her name.'

'Her name is Léonie,' said Tante Celestine.

'Léonie,' I murmured, 'Léonie.'

'And after he says her name,' said the jester, 'what then should he say?'

'Fifty francs, please.'

'You want me to ask her for money?' I said.

'She means,' said the jester, 'that you should put fifty francs in the box in the church.'

I went downstairs immediately and did so.

'All right, Tante,' said the jester when I returned, 'continue.'

'When the full moon is shining on her face,' said Tante Celestine, 'he should stand in front of her and say, "Léonie, I am here."'

'"Léonie, I am here." I think I can remember that,' I said. 'What then?'

'What then, Tante?' said the jester.

'Then he must watch carefully because the moment will flicker like a fish turning in the water and the stone sphinx of Léonie's public self will smile. Then the Léonie of hot blood and willing flesh will separate herself from the stone and leap to the ground. When that happens he must very quickly move in behind the flickering to the moment under the moment; he must climb over the gate and into the garden of his desire where he will find that Léonie who is the sphinx-woman of herself.'

'Very quickly behind the flickering, I've got it. When's the next full moon?'

'Tonight,' said the jester.

'There's a destiny in these things. What time does it rise?'

'Minutes and hours are nothing to me. Phone the Observatoire.'

'OK, I'll do that. What's your name?'

'Gaspard.'

'Many thanks, Gaspard and Tante Celestine. I'll let you know what happens.'

'We'll be here,' said Gaspard.

I left another fifty francs in the box in the church and this time I lingered to look at the polychromed statue of Sainte-Marie L'Égyptienne holding the three loaves with which she went into the desert. When her clothes wore out she made do with her knee-length blonde hair. The statue was showing a lot of leg but the hair was keeping her decent and for added security the sculptor had provided a stone apron. The shapeliness of her thighs accentuated the somewhat sour piety of her face. I doubted that the sexual act had ever been one of alchemical transformation for her.

According to my *Oxford Dictionary of Saints* this Marie had been a whore in Alexandria from the age of twelve. When she was twenty-nine she joined a pilgrimage to Jerusalem, paying her way by sleeping with the sailors. When she arrived she was prevented by an invisible force from entering the church. 'Lifting her eyes to an ikon of the Blessed Virgin, she was told to go over the Jordan where she would find rest.' That's when she bought the three loaves and went into the desert where she spent the rest of her life living on dates and berries and being 'divinely instructed in the Christian faith'. She met a monk called Zosimus from whom she hoped to receive communion the following Maundy Thursday but when he turned up he found her dead. A lion helped him bury her. This story depressed me. Sainte-Marie and I had no conversation: she had nothing to say to me and I had nothing to say to her. I wished that I hadn't allowed her into my field of vision, I didn't want her standing in front of Léonie in my mind.

I went back to the hotel, phoned the Observatoire, and was told that moonrise would be at 20:01 – more than five hours to get through. I didn't want to see Léonie before then and I didn't want to take in anything new but I was unwilling to wait passively in my room. I left the hotel and walked without taking much notice of where I was until I found myself in the Place des Vosges, boxed in by a four-sided frieze of stylised leaf-and-branch patterns printed on the air with a background of buildings. Figures on benches, like rocks in a Japanese garden, made islands in the clean gravel. There may have been a ringing of bells, perhaps not. The minutes roared and bellowed like minotaurs, the tides moved with the unseen moon, years passed, I grew old, and after a long time there was twilight with rain.

I walked back along Saint-Antoine and the Rue de Rivoli. The streets glistened with a constant susurration of colour and motion in which dark figures hurried through labyrinths and fireworks of traffic and the moment that was not yet. The sky offered no clarity, only rain. The moon did not exist, there had never been a moon, there never would be a moon, the idea of a moon was nothing to be taken seriously.

At 19:52 I manifested myself at the Rue de Rivoli end of the Avenue du Général Lemonnier. Léonie was at the other end of the avenue and could not be seen from where I was. I felt that it would be improper to show myself before the time dictated by Tante Celestine, and with the weather as it was there was no certainty that the moon would appear at all this night. There was nothing to do but maintain a state of readiness while awaiting further developments.

The rain was gentle but my jacket was not waterproof and although April was only one day away this evening seemed more like November. Colour and motion continued all around me; people with maps in their hands rushed past me to hurl themselves upon Paris; the Rue de Rivoli was euphoric with reflections and the sound of engines, the lights and the hiss of tyres disdained my silence, my stillness.

It was at this moment that the death of Général Lemonnier approached me. It was without form but it was as big as a church and while not making itself visible it made everything else go away so that there was nothing before me but it and nothing around us but silence. The story of this death appears on a bronze plaque on the end of the terrace wall on which Léonie crouches. The top of her head is about four metres above the ground and as you face her you see, reading from the top down, Léonie; plinth; plaque; street sign. The plaque says:

AU GÉNÉRAL EMILE LEMONNIER
Commandant la 3ème Brigade de la Division du Tonkin
LE DIX MARS 1945, CAPTURÉ À LANG-SON PAR L'ENNEMI,
À BOUT DE MUNITIONS, A REFUSÉ PAR DEUX FOIS
DE SIGNER UNE CAPITULATION TOTALE,
A PRÉFÉRÉ AVOIR LA TÊTE TRANCHÉE
PLUTÔT QUE DE FORFAIRE À L'HONNEUR,
DEMEURERA DANS L'HISTOIRE

My Night with Léonie

COMME UN EXEMPLE SAISISSANT DE CE QUE SONT
LA VOLONTÉ ET LA CARACTÈRE FRANÇAIS
(Citation posthume – Extrait)

Below it is the street sign in white letters on a Prussian Blue ground:

1e Arrt.

AVENUE
DU GÉNÉRAL
LEMONNIER
1893–1945

MORT IN INDOCHINE

The death of Général Lemonnier spoke not in the manner of Léonie and Gaspard and Tante Celestine but inaudibly to the mind. Do you matter? it enquired.

Not at all, I said. And yet . . .

And yet what?

One does one's possible, yes?

The death of Général Lemonnier seemed to relax a little.

You and the sphinx, I said, you're not . . . ?

There is nothing between us, said the death of Général Lemonnier. She's young, I'm old; I was old even at Thermopylae. She's modern, she . . .

What? I said. She what?

Nothing. You're in love with her?

Yes.

Good luck.

'Thank you,' I said aloud as the world returned with lights and noise and traffic. The time was 19:59 and the sky was dead, touched up with a pinkish glow as by an embalmer. There had never been stars, there had never been a moon.

I ran down the avenue – I didn't want to be early but I didn't want to be late in case the sky should suddenly come to life and produce a moon. I arrived in front of Léonie's terrace at 20:01 just as the seven Japanese gentlemen came round the corner of the Quai des Tuileries.

They were all wearing black waterproof tracksuits and black plimsolls and carrying various black cases of a technical nature; at first glance one couldn't say whether they meant to shoot a film, transmit messages by satellite, or rob a bank. When they saw me they gave only the briefest of nods and the smallest of smiles. They didn't look at Léonie at all.

Ignoring the rain and working with military snap while they exchanged short sharp words they set up what appeared to be a weather station – at least I recognised the anemometer and the balloon that was inflated from a gas cylinder and sent aloft with an instrument packet and a radio transmitter. Next out of the cases was something possibly deriving from a sextant, an astrolabe and an infra-red sniperscope. This apparatus was mounted on a tripod and one of the Japanese took sights of the dense overcast and called out his readings while another entered the data on a calculator. A wireless receiver was deployed as well as several laptop computers and all of the seven became very busy, those who were not operating a scientific device or piece of communication equipment making notes in electronic notebooks or calculating with their calculators or computing with their computers, the dim red glow of the screens illuminating the intensity of their faces.

After about fifteen minutes they exchanged more short sharp words, packed up their gear, and disappeared round the corner whence they had come. What had they done? What did they know that I didn't? I had no idea but I was full of a fear that I didn't want to put into words.

I had avoided looking at Léonie while all this was going on and I didn't look at her now – it seemed unlucky to do so and I sensed that the stone of her was not in an interactive mode. There was still the possibility that the sky might clear so I leant against the wall of the terrace with my back to her and my face towards the south-eastern quarter of the sky in which I hoped there would eventually be a moon.

The rain continued and I fell into a reverie or possibly a delirium in which my wetness became a river that carried me to the sea where I swam with singing whales and silent turtles following their submarine destinies. Below us in tropical waters mantis shrimps with strange compound eyes looked at colours invisible to humans while the great-winged wandering albatross soared and swooped above the southern ocean or slept rocking on the waves. Under the rain and over the sea spread the shadow of Saint-Germain l'Auxerrois and the deaths in their thousands that answered its bell while a mermaid Sainte-Marie with her long hair streaming behind her swam with three loaves of coral in her hands.

I must have been asleep because I woke up to the sound of Léonie's name followed by something in Japanese. It was 22:45; the rain had stopped, the clouds had parted and the white moon floated serenely above the domes and spires and gargoyles of Paris. I stepped away from the terrace and looked up; the moonlight was full on the face of the sphinx but the stone was empty – Léonie was elsewhere. From behind the locked gate of the Jardin des Tuileries came cries of pleasure, ululations of ecstasy, words in Japanese. Silence, then I saw one of the seven Japanese gentlemen leaving the garden. He climbed over the gate as lithe as a cat and dropped to the ground as another of the seven came round the corner of the Quai des Tuileries.

I looked up and saw that Léonie was once more present in the statue on the plinth; the stone was now responsive as the next man looked up and said, 'Léonie ... ' and the rest in Japanese. The sphinx smiled voluptuously, I saw the moment flicker like a fish turning in the water, saw the stone go empty as the living lion-woman leapt down from her plinth, tearing off her formal Egyptian headdress to let her long red hair flame out behind her. O God, the tawniness of her long lion-body and the ivory of her woman-body, the savage flaunt of her breasts and haunches and lashing tail, the invitation of her red mouth and white teeth and wild green eyes. I had fallen in love with the statue and had imagined the stone become flesh but the reality of her put my imagination to shame. Her more than animal, more than human sexuality was so transcendently elemental, was such a startling and unwordable mystery that it utterly overwhelmed all reason and intellect. The brilliant strangeness of her printed itself on my eyes and I understood then how the idea of the sphinx had persisted century after century in successive minds and would persist as long as there was a single mind to contain it.

Only for a fraction of a second was Léonie-as-herself visible, then she disappeared into the garden while the empty statue kept watch on the plinth as the new man vaulted the fence like a champion. I turned away, went round the corner into the Quai des Tuileries, walked past the six Japanese who waited there (the first man had now joined the end of the queue), returned their nods and smiles, and made my way slowly back to the hotel. I drew the curtains, had a hot shower, and crept into bed around midnight without looking out of the window.

I woke up the next morning sneezing and sniffling and opened the curtains. There they were, Gaspard and his headless partner and Tante Celestine. 'Good day,' said Gaspard. 'It goes?'

'You lousy pimp,' I said. 'Why didn't you tell me she was a whore?'

'Whore!' said Gaspard. 'She's a saint, that Léonie. Have you any idea how much it costs to keep this church in repair, how inflation has raised the price of everything from candles to roof tiles? You think your night with her wasn't worth the piddling fifty francs you paid? You want your money back because she's not a virgin? You watch how you talk

to me, arsehole – I can easily arrange for something to fall
on you.'

'Kill,' said Tante Celestine. 'Kill the son of a bitch, Gaspard. Drop your head on him and teach him a lesson.'

I closed the window and turned away. At breakfast the
Japanese and I smiled and nodded. Not one of them was
sniffling or sneezing. After breakfast I walked to where
Léonie crouched in her public mode. The sunlight, as always,
sang its little song:

> This, yes this, how strange it is that this
> is this, is this, is this, is this . . ,

This time she spoke first. 'Hey, big shot,' she said, 'where
were you last night? Lots of talk but no action, eh?'

'I seemed to have arrived a little late.'

'And you didn't want to be the last in the queue? Life is
like that, my old – so many wanting the same thing and so
little time to serve them all.'

'But you were so different when we spoke that first
time, you even said . . . '

'I said what you wanted to hear. I sensed that you wanted
to be my first, wanted to awaken the wildness in me, wanted
me to open my little mouth to you. Listen, don't be cross –
come back tonight and I'll be a virgin for you. I'll dress up
as a nun, you'll like that. For fifty francs more I'll beat you
with a little whip, yes? Come on, my gallant, be a sport.'

'I'm leaving today. Adieu.' I walked away.

'Don't say *adieu*, say *au revoir*,' she called after me.

'Adieu,' I said again. One may be a fool but one has one's
standards, one draws the line, however faintly, somewhere.

When I got back to London I was going to change my
French money but then I didn't. I like seeing the notes and
the coins on my desk; sometimes I put my passport on top of
them and the red-covered *Plan de Paris par Arrondissement*
beside them. I like the way they look together, I like the way
they feel in my hand.

Schwartz

I'd been stuck for months – no ideas that went anywhere. Then suddenly things started moving again. I always have music going while I work, and when I put on *Miles Davis Blue Note Vol. 1* that morning it sounded different, as if there were good places ahead. I did almost two pages of something that looked promising and I scribbled notes with ideas for later.

After lunch I thought, things being in such good shape, why didn't I go to Tottenham Court Road and get some blank four-hour videotapes, then drop in at Virgin for a couple of Jimmy Smith cassettes and see if they had Sun Ra – I liked his rendition of 'Round about Midnight'.

In the underground I read the Bernard Malamud short story, 'The Jewbird', shaking my head and thinking, What a writer. He makes it look so easy, as if all you have to do is let good things come into your head and then just tell them however they want to be told. When I came out of the train in Tottenham Court Road tube station there was a short white saxophonist playing 'Ornithology' like a suitor trying to bend the bow of Odysseus. I gave him 20p.

I bought the videotapes at Hi-Fi Care and then I went to Great Russell Street for a look at the bookshops before going to Virgin. In the entrance of Collet's Chinese I saw on the wall by the door a handsome chart, THE CHINESE

RADICALS: *The 214 Index Characters of the Kang Hsi Dictionary.* It was startling in its beauty and compactness. Here, in ten rows, were single characters for *Rain, Moon, Evil, Mountain* – all manner of concrete and conceptual words with which to image a whole world. The characters were grouped according to the number of brush strokes that composed them. They seemed magical, as if the physical act of making the strokes in black ink on white paper had the power of calling up the physical being of what the character represented. Some of the sequences seemed already to be telling stories: in a three-stroke row, character 37, *Great*, was followed by *Woman, Child, Roof, Inch, Small, Lame, crooked*, and *Corpse*. In a five-stroke row, character 109, *Eye*, was followed by *Lance, Arrow, Stone*, and *Spirit*.

I ran my finger over the characters from *Great* to *Corpse*; in the whiteness between the black brush strokes there seemed a distant place, another time, a face not clearly seen. Geography doesn't apply, I thought. *Great* was a man-shape (why great?), a plain, bare, forked creature moving towards *Woman* who, waiting with outstretched arms, took his man-shape into herself. *Child* followed, with a hook like an anchor. Did they all live under one (very modest) *Roof*? No, the dwelling was *Inch*, it was *Small*, nothing that would hold *Great*. *Child* (a boy, judging by its similarity to *Great*), was *Lame, crooked*, then *Corpse*. Sad. After *Corpse* came *Sprout*, the grass growing on the child's grave. Then *Mountain*, then *Stream*, pointed ripples. Did *Mountain* and *Stream* have any significance for *Great*? He returned to his *Work*, his concerns of *Self*. All this in characters 37 to 49 on the chart.

I came back from wherever I'd been, bought a copy of the chart and left the shop. As I continued east on Great Russell Street I became aware of something a little behind me and to my left and I heard a smacking sound as of wet feet on the pavement. When I turned, whatever I saw out of the corner of my eye was blurred and gone before I had a proper look. I decided not to go into Probsthain's, the next bookshop, but crossed the road and headed for the British Museum.

People eating ice-cream strolled in and out of the gates while behind me the wet footfalls continued. On the museum steps in the August sunlight sat girls from everywhere with beckoning bare legs inviting the approacher to the darkness within, the coolness of marble, the excitement of stone, the persistence of ideas. As I went up the steps I didn't look behind me but I still heard the smack of wet feet. How could feet stay wet for such a long time on hot dry paving? I turned suddenly but saw only the girls from everywhere.

I went inside. I didn't know what I was looking for but I'd know it when I saw it. I didn't want huge winged bulls from Persepolis with bearded human faces, I didn't want the lion-hunt reliefs in the Assyrian Saloon, and I didn't want either colossal or non-colossal Egyptian statues. I looked in on the Elgin Marbles but they were of no use to me this time. I went up the stairs, drifted urgently through South Arabia, Nimrud Ivories, and Syria, turned left at Pottery and Small Objects, headed north through Daily Life and Coptic Art, west through Temporary Prints and Drawings, and found myself in Oriental Antiquities standing in front of a black stone lion. Oh, I said. You.

There wasn't much light on its blackness, the lion was mostly in shadow where it sat on its plinth, somewhat bigger than a large dog and showing its teeth in a ready grimace. There was no air between the front legs and the back legs, the whole lion was one with the stone, its form compact and simplified, its posture humped and ready; the shape of it was the shape of readiness, more mass than detail – there was hardly any detail, only the black stone bulk of the lion manifesting its steadfast willingness to encounter whatever might come at it. This was not a lion by artifice, it had lived unseen in the stone until the sculptor's chisel took away its hiddenness and the lion, grimacing, was exposed to view.

FIGURE OF A GUARDIAN LION FROM A TOMB AVENUE, said the card – SUNG DYNASTY, AD 960–1279.

'Don't touch the exhibit,' said the guard as I lifted my hands to the lion's shoulders.

I moved away and looked at the T'ang Dynasty horses for a while. When the guard was elsewhere I went back to the lion. I had my Walkman in my shoulder bag, in it a cassette of the Thelonious Monk quartet on its 1961 European tour – Charlie Rouse, tenor sax; John Ore, bass; Frankie Dunlop, drums. The tape was at the end of 'Round about Midnight' and just about to begin 'Blue Monk'. I put the headphones on the lion's head and started the music. I had my left hand on the lion's head, and when I felt the stone begin to hum I took off the headphones.

The lion blurred, the floor shook a little and several people, noticing perhaps some disturbance in the air, turned to look as we walked away. On the plinth there was still a lion that could be seen and touched but the stone was empty.

We went down the stairs, crossed the crowded and echoing space to the entrance, and went out to the brilliant sunlight and the girls from everywhere, now seen from behind or in profile. As we passed through them I looked back. Their motion was arrested, their voices were swallowed up in silence; the girls from everywhere, dropping all pretence of the ordinary, became shadowy in the sunlight, became mystery.

I want to hear the rest of that music, said the invisible incorporeal essence of the black stone lion as we turned down Great Russell Street towards Tottenham Court Road. We talked mind to mind, no one else could hear us.

I can't very well hang headphones on empty air, I said.

If you put them on your head I can listen through you, said the lion.

I don't want to. There's something else I'm listening for.

What's that?

Something following me.

Is that why you came to me?

I don't know.

Yes, you do. You don't like being followed, it bothers you?

Well, I'd rather not be followed by anything too blurry.

Don't worry about it.

Why not?

There are blurry things following everybody, that's the human condition.

How come I never noticed this one before, then?

Nobody can notice everything, it's too much, it would drive you crazy.

Anyhow I'd like to keep listening for it if you don't mind.

Please yourself. Who are you at present?

I'm who I've always been, Harry Stone.

Always is a long time. Before you were Stone you were Stein, right?

Right.

And before that?

Unborn.

Unborn as Stein, you mean.

Whatever. And you?

Schwartz. No first name, just Schwartz.

Same name as Malamud's Jewbird.

There's a lot of it about.

Odd name for a Chinese lion.

Actually I'm Jewish.

How can a Sung Dynasty tomb guardian be Jewish?

You know how it is with immigrants – we get the dirty jobs.

What's dirty about being a tomb guardian?

It's a matter of whose tomb you're guarding, isn't it.

And whose tomb were you guarding?

A cabinet minister's. I'm still on duty, it's a permanent post.

You're a long way from China.

So are you, but geography doesn't apply in these matters. Whose tomb do you think I'm guarding?

I've no idea. How could I?

I was assigned to the Minister of Drains and Gutters. Does that ring a bell?

No. Should it?

Yes, it should.

Why's that?

Because the Minister of Drains and Gutters is you and it's your tomb I'm guarding, that's why.

My tomb!

Well, I say 'tomb' because that's what one says. What I actually look after is the idea of you. The world is a fabric of ideas; each thing lives in a particular idea that lives in it. These ideas aren't always what you might expect. Take such a thing as a roof, for example; perhaps the idea of it is not the shelter it gives but the shelter it doesn't give. Or a mountain, the idea of it might not be the immensity of it but the smallness of what isn't mountain. Or a stream, the idea of it might not be the constant motion of the water but a moment of it that stops and does not move on. The idea of you, of course, is free flow.

Free flow! But I'm not the Minister of Drains and Gutters.

All right, so maybe you've taken up something new. I wonder if I can guess what you are now? Something in the arts, am I right?

I'm a writer.

Well, there you are, it's the same thing, isn't it.

What's the same thing?

What you do. A Minister of Drains and Gutters has to keep things flowing freely in and out and so does a writer, only the writer does it with ideas and the minister does it with other things. So it's not really a big change for you.

Listen, Schwartz, I said ... Then I heard the wet feet on the pavement again. Listen, do you hear that?

Certainly I hear it.

Well, why is it following me? What does it want?

Don't you know?

No, I don't.

Why don't you ask her then?

Her?

It, then, if you like. But it's the it of her.

Of whom? I thought. But I didn't really want to know. Why can't I see this it of her? I said. Every time I turn around there's only a blur that I see out of the corner of my eye.

She was always very humble, you know. She probably isn't quite able to face you.

Maybe I'm not able to face her either.

Why not?

Maybe I just don't want to.

Why not?

Why don't you stop asking questions and do a little guarding, I wanted to say but didn't. Life is hard enough without extra bother, I said lamely. We were at Tottenham Court Road tube station then; we went down the stairs and I bought a ticket for Schwartz, I didn't want to cheat anybody in any way on this particular day.

In the corridor we passed a tall black saxophonist with dreadlocks and a tremendous red and yellow and blue cap like a knitted Greek Orthodox church dome. He was playing 'Blue Monk' with a Monk tape for backing. I gave him 20p and Schwartz insisted on stopping to listen.

I wanted to get home; the dusk was beginning to gather, the day was ending. You can hear 'Blue Monk' at my place, I said.

Not as played by this strange holy man on his wonderful machine, said Schwartz. This is the free flow of the present moment.

Do you always have to go with the flow?

Yes.

So we stood and listened while the rush hour passed around us. The saxophonist seemed suspicious of our attention but carried on playing nonetheless.

In due course we arrived at the platform and waited for our train. After a few minutes the black air of the tunnel rushed towards us and the rails began to wince as a distant rumble grew louder.

Schwartz growled as the waiting crowd pressed forward towards the edge where white light slid along the rails below us.

Why are you growling? I said.

The air is full of trouble.

That's our train, we have to ride in it; it's part of the free flow of the present moment.

The darkness opened and like a shriek the train filled up the tunnel, the doors slid back, and we got on. Once inside, we stood in the crush without talking, Schwartz occupying no space whatever. Strange, I thought, as our carriage shook and rattled through the darkness: here I am travelling with a Sung Dynasty tomb guardian who likes Thelonious Monk and probably nobody knows it but me. I looked with new interest at the faces packed around me, wondering whom some of these people might be travelling with; wondering, indeed, whether anyone ever travelled alone. Sometimes I thought I saw the blurred face, sometimes not.

Under the fluorescent brightness that was neither day nor night I saw in the faces around me the darkening of the unseen sky. With the fading of the day came the little tribunal of the dusk. I sat at the bench as judge and I stood in the dock as the accused. No one spoke for the defence because there was no defence.

The doors of the past opened and they came in, the faces and the places, the words spoken and unspoken, the roads travelled, the tears and the partings.

At certain times in your life you did what you did, I the judge said to the accused. You, Harold Stone, did this and this and this.

Yes, I said to the judge, I did.

How do you find? I, the judge, said to the faces and

the places, the words, the roads, the tears, the partings.
Guilty.
How do you find? I said to the accused.
Guilty, I answered from the dock.
You are condemned to regret. Do you so condemn?
I so condemn.
Do you recognise the power and the authority of regret?
I do.
Followers will be appointed, those who pursue and those who exact what is due. Do you accept this?

The doors opened. Schwartz and I and others left the train, walked up the stairs and out under pinky-orange streetlamps and a violet sky. Behind us came the footfalls.

At home we sat in the living room with none of the lamps switched on. Twilight filled the room like dark waters from far away. I put 'Blue Monk' on the tape deck. The music impeccably shaped its angles in the darkening room, at the same time sculpting the duplicate lion of itself and reproducing moments lived silently in real time by real people: the breathing of the musicians and the audience, the beating of their hearts and the circulation of their blood were in the moments imitated by the magnetised particles on the tape; if there had been a fly sitting on Monk's hat while he played, its tiny presence was copied in the recorded music; if it had been raining at the time of the concert, the unseen wet and shining streets, the reflections of headlamps and tail-lights, streetlamps and traffic-lights, the unheard hiss of tyres and the sound of the rain, all were in the simulacrum concert on the tape. Was the double helix of each of us, I wondered, a recording of all the lives before us?

Who was she? I said to Schwartz.

In the light of the streetlamp outside the window Schwartz made himself visible, black and humped and grimacing in the room that was dark now except for the little red diodes on the amplifier and the tape deck. I don't remember her name, he said. She was a small woman and very humble. She had never been outside her village in the remote province where she lived. She had never seen anyone so splendidly dressed as you, so important and with a retinue of servants and soldiers and carrying documents from the Emperor. Did you make promises?

It wasn't I. You're confusing me with someone else.

Does it matter?

What kind of sophistry is that? Of course it matters. Why don't you find the Minister of Drains and Gutters and tell him all this that you're telling me?

Bodies rot, spirits fade. It's been a very long time.

So you admit you've got the wrong man!

No, you're the right man. Even if you're not the one who was the Minister of Drains and Gutters, you're the one for whom I guard and preserve the idea of free flow.

It's the idea that you're guarding, not me.

Not you but the idea. We're both Jews, you and I; we are of the people who make no images of God; we are of the people for whom God is idea and Idea is god. Do you accept that?

Uncertain, I stood silent in the dock.

Look at me.

I looked at him, looked through the darkness into the black stone of his eyes that pierced me like lances, like arrows, going from the spirit of the stone into the stone of my spirit.

There were others before you, said Schwartz, and there will be others after you. How much does it matter who did what? What was done was done and must flow freely. The woman waited and you never returned; there was a child and he died. She waited until the second winter, then she walked by a mountain stream, walked by the deep and rushing water.

And now?

She would like not to be alone any more, she asks only a little look of recognition, a little word of welcome and affection.

One more follower.
Surely you can take on one more?
All right then. Let her come.

'Blue Monk', always full of lift, seemed to lift a little more. The footsteps, when I heard them, sounded different, as if her feet were dry now.

The Raven

One says 'a black time', but actually the black of things is all kinds of colours. Sometimes it's the grey rainlight in an empty room; sometimes it's the sound of one's own footsteps under yellow streetlamps; sometimes it's an unaccompanied cello from a long time ago. It was difficult to understand the reality of my days, that this was now my life that would last until my death, that I had closed a door and gone, that there was no going back, that no one was there any more. No one was there because you don't just leave people, you leave a time. And the time wasn't there any more.

I wanted to talk to somebody about the black so I went down into the underground, came up out of it on the long and windy escalator at Camden Town, walked up Parkway to Regent's Park, followed a footpath through green distances and the autumnal shouts of football players, and turned into a road in which a squad of trotting men in red T-shirts and green shorts came towards me, their leader chanting words to which they responded. The words were indistinct, probably not:

> There was a man, his name was Jack,
> he tried to swim across the black.
> THE BLACK WAS DEEP, THE BLACK WAS WIDE,
> HE NEVER REACHED THE OTHER SIDE.

The road took me to the Zoo entrance, where I entered, went past the apes and a little white clock tower and found the ravens. There were two of them perching on a sawed-off dead tree in their cage. When I took some grapes out of a bag one of the ravens opened its wings and the whole outspread blackness of the bird suddenly appeared in front of me. Standing on well-worn and polished black feet, it folded its wings and stuck its bill through the chain-link mesh of the cage. It was a large black bill of clerical aspect, the upper mandible hooked over the lower with a long curving point that was like a fingernail that needed trimming. A little yellow sign on the cage showed the silhouette of a hand with a large piece bitten out, so I sidled away from the raven and dropped a grape through the wire mesh.

The raven picked up the grape neatly between its upper and lower mandibles, walked a little way off with an old-man walk, placed the grape on the concrete floor, tore it into three pieces, and ate them one at a time. Then it went to its bath, a circular concavity in the floor; it sipped some water, lifted its head and stretched out its neck as it swallowed, and came back to the wire-mesh. Its wet throat-feathers were like a beard, its purple-blue blackness was as precise as an engraving, its shining black eye when it blinked showed a clear bluish-white disc like a little round mirror of scepticism.

How's it going? I said to it, not speaking aloud but with my mind.

Well, you know, said the raven, also not speaking aloud, there's not a lot happening here.

The cage was small, with neighbours on both sides. I think there was some kind of vulture in the cage to the left, some exotic corvid to the right. From time to time the vulture flapped its wings and lifted itself off its branch, then settled down again. The October day was warm and humid, people carried their coats and jackets over their arms. Someone stood next to me and pointed to the raven and said to a child, 'See how tame it is.' I looked down at the child, a boy of three or four. His face was pale and sticky like a bun that had been standing in the sun. His expression was doubtful, his eyes wild. The sky was grey, dead leaves rattled on the paving, in the distance something screamed.

How can you live without flying? I said to the raven. How do you get through the days? How do you not go crazy?

The raven looked at me for a while, the little round eye-mirror blinked like a camera shutter. Lots of people live without flying, it said.

But you used to have the whole sky to move around in

Wait a minute, said the raven

What?

How do I know I'm not talking to myself? Maybe I'm just imagining this conversation.

I've been thinking that very same thought, I said. Tell me what to do to show that I'm receiving you.

Hold out your arms and flap them up and down.

I held out my arms and flapped them up and down.

'What's that man doing?' said a passing child to its mother.

'Perhaps he's trying to get above himself,' she said.

I've given you a sign, I said to the raven. How about you? Walk in a circle round your bath if it's really you speaking to me.

With its old-man walk the raven slowly walked around the bath. Then it came back to where I stood. You were saying, it said. Its voice in my mind had changed: it was all around me in vast and reverberant diapason, as if rebounding from the face of a black escarpment that ringed the horizon under a grey and primordial sky. It was a giant voice of supernatural power, and a thrill of fear went through me as the raven grew before my eyes. The cage and the zoo seemed to have faded away; the raven loomed over me like a black cliff walking towards me on well-worn and polished black feet in the grey October afternoon. How could I ever have been such a fool as to speak to it as if I were its equal?

43

The immense raven flashed its eye-mirror in which I saw only blankness. Its voice filled the sky. You were saying, it said.

How do you not go crazy? I whispered in my mind.

I have a lot to do, I'm busy all the time, chorused the massed echoes from the black escarpment.

What is it that you do?

I do the black.

Of course, the black. I'd come for the express purpose of talking to the raven about that very thing and I'd forgotten all about it. When you say 'the black', I said, you mean . . . ?

Different things at different times.

And when you do the black, how do you do it?

I just go with it.

How do you do that, how do you just go with it?

All kinds of ways and very, very far sometimes.

How far? I was looking into the raven's left eye when I said that. Then the mirror flashed and I was in that eye looking out. Around me the vast blackness of the bird opened and lifted and the earth fell away below us, all the feeble constructions of humankind and the smoke of its engines blurring into dimness and distance as we rose above the grey sky and into the brilliant clarity of the blue dome in which the present curved endlessly upon itself to compass past and future.

Up we flew, high, high into the blue dome, then whistling down in a dizzying black-winged rush we shot the long, long curve past faces huge and tiny on the flickering screen of memory, faces in the shadows, in the light, lips shaping words remembered and forgotten in the moving gleams of time, the wavering of candlelight, the whispering of gold watches, the boom of tower clocks, the fading ink of letters tied with faded ribbons; faces wheeling with horsemen and battles and cannon, marching with armies, screaming in burning cities, drowning in shipwrecks and the thunder of the wild black ocean; palimpsested voices, distant figures and the changing

44

colours of processions, plagues, migrations, ruins, standing stones, cave drawings, jungles, deserts, dust, meteorites, dinosaurs, giant ferns, volcanoes, floods, blue-green algae, silence, the grey rainlight in an empty room, the sound of my footsteps under yellow streetlamps, and an unaccompanied cello from a long time ago.

That's rather a long way to come for not very much, I said to the raven.

With this kind of thing it's always trial and error, said the raven. We can go a little further if you want to.

We might as well give it a try.

All right, then, here we go.

Down, down we allowed blackly through the silence and the rainlight and the footsteps and the streetlamps and the unaccompanied cello to a dim and smoking red that seethed and cracked and bubbled and was veined with golden rivulets of lava. Down, down through that red to a dimmer red, a deeper silence, an older stillness.

Where are we? I said.

In the black.

This isn't black, it's red.

Sometimes the black is red. We have to walk from here.

I looked down at the raven's worn and polished black feet. They seemed far, far away. I imagined the raven sitting down on the edge of its bed and lacing them up every morning. Far below me in the dim, dim red the raven's left foot moved and then its right. Is it very far? I said.

It's where we are when we come to it.

The raven's old-man walk made its head lurch from side to side so that I swung like a pendulum in a black clock. We didn't talk, there wasn't anything to say. Sometimes the red was smooth, sometimes it was gritty underfoot. Some kind of music would have been suitable for the gait of the raven but there was no music. Do you come here often? I said.

It isn't always here when I come.

Well, yes, I could understand that. There were no landmarks at all and the densities and textures of the red were probably unreliable. Time and silence receded before us steadily until they became the same as they were before. We were in a cavern dimly lit by the red and flickering light of our mind, the raven's and mine.

Here, we said.

What?

Here, here, here. Our voice had become many voices, voices without number, tiny and great. The raven was no longer a raven, raven, raven, raven. Nor was I what I had been; we were without form, we were not yet alive: tiny, tiny dancing giants looming greatly in uncertain shapes and dwindling in the shadows; fast asleep and dancing in the dim red caverns of sleep.

Through agelong dimnesses of red we danced and sang incessantly the long song of our sorting: yes and no we sang in silence, grouping and dispersing and regrouping in the circles and the spirals of the sleep-dance. Many, many, sang the many of us, all of everything the same.

We danced the red until it became red-orange; then we danced red-orange in the sameness of our unbeing; in the caverns of sleep we danced orange and orange-yellow while the mountains cooled under the long rains and the deeps filled up with oceans. When the yellow came and the yellow-green it seemed that green and blue-green were only a matter of time.

Same, same, sang we tiny, tiny dancing giants through all the colours of the years: all of us the same.

What us? said some.

All of us, said others.

All of us what?

All of us the same.

Same what?

Same us.

What us?

46

All of us.

And so on through revolving repetitions over hundreds of thousands of millions of years. From time to time there were attempts to move the discussion on to new ground but always it reverted to the same revolving repetitions. Little by little we were losing energy, and although I had at that time no identity I was becoming more and more impatient with the apparent unwillingness of my fellow tiny, tiny dancing giants to pull themselves together so that we could make something of ourselves. My particles were beginning to scatter when, with a tremendous effort, I said, Un . . .

Un what? said the others.

Un the same, I said. Unsame.

Same, insisted many.

Unsame, said more and more. Over the next hundreds of thousands of millions of years this alternating challenge and response slowly developed in us a forward motion; we could feel ourselves moving out of unbeing into a new state. SAME, UNSAME, we chanted all together as we surged forward through shallow seas and primordial salts into the blue-green algae of our beginning.

Having begun, we pressed forward through floods, volcanoes, giant ferns, dinosaurs, meteorites, dust, deserts, jungles, cave drawings, standing stones, ruins, migrations, plagues, the changing colours of processions and distant figures, palimpsested voices, faces huge and tiny on the flickering screen of memory, faces drowning in shipwrecks and the thunder of the wild black ocean, screaming in burning cities, marching with armies, wheeling with horsemen and battles and cannon; faces in the shadows, in the light, lips shaping words remembered and forgotten in the moving gleams of time, the whispering of gold watches, the boom of tower clocks, the fading ink of letters tied with faded ribbons. Nothing stopped us, and in time we arrived at the grey rainlight in the empty room, the sound of my footsteps under yellow streetlamps, and the unaccompanied cello from long ago where the raven stood on its well-worn and polished black feet looking at me through the chain-link mesh of the cage.

I wanted, said the raven, speaking to me with its mind, to ask you about the black.

What can I tell you? I said. It's different things at different times but it's more or less the same.

I left the Zoo and walked back the way I'd come. When I turned into the road where the trotting men had chanted I saw them coming towards me again. Again their words were indistinct, probably not:

> There is a thing, it has no name,
> this thing is everywhere the same.
> THIS THING IS DEEP, THIS THING IS WIDE,
> IT HASN'T GOT A FARTHER SIDE.

I walked down Parkway, went down the long and windy escalator at Camden Town, came up out of the underground at my desk but didn't sit down at it. I lay down on the couch, fell asleep, dreamed that I was writing, and woke up unable to remember what I'd written.

The Colour of Love

Lavinia's letter began as if she was picking up a conversation we'd left off only a moment ago:

Cannaregio 4273
Venezia
16 November 1988

Dear Harry,
    Ten years ago I was in the Accademia standing in front of Giorgione's *La Tempesta* when a man I'd never seen before came and stood beside me. He seemed not to be looking at the naked woman suckling the baby in the foreground but above and beyond her. I knew that he was going to speak to me and I knew by the hang of his face that he was going to speak English. 'Have you ever seen storks over the Bosporus?' he said.
    'No. Have you?'
    'No, but I think about them sometimes. The Bosporus is one of their migration routes. I can see them in my mind, high in the air . . . ' Long pause.
    'Go on.'
    'Like great-winged thoughts.'
    'You weren't sure about saying that aloud.'
    'No, I wasn't.'

'You think that's a stork on the roof of that building in the background?'

'Definitely.'

'Doesn't look all that much like a stork, it's hardly more than the ghost of a bird. The sky is so threatening.'

'There's always danger but "the stork in the heaven knoweth her appointed times; and the turtle and the swallow and the crane observe the time of their coming . . . "'

'And you think this is the appointed time for that particular stork?'

'Yes, I do.'

'Maybe that's the stork that brought the baby she's been left with.' I didn't want him to be too successful with his quotation from Jeremiah.

'What makes you think she's been left?'

'Well, there she is by the roadside, starkers. She looks as if she's waiting for someone to come along and take her and the baby in and that chap on the left seems to be considering it.'

Nonetheless he'd got to me with the stork, those lines have always been mystical for me. We left the Accademia, went halfway across the wooden bridge, and stood looking into the sea mist towards a ghostly Santa Maria della Salute and listening to foghorns . . .

There's more but I'll leave that till later. No one's heard from Lavinia Haworth since that letter arrived with her box-easel on 28 November 1988, almost two years ago, sent to me by a priest from Santa Maria dei Miracoli in Venice. 'I have followed the instructions of the English lady as far as I was able,' he says in his letter. 'From a distance I have seen her painting on the Fondamenta Sanudo but later she was not there.'

I own only one painting by Lavinia that I bought in 1987.

I couldn't afford a Haworth now, the cheapest of them go for five thousand pounds. My painting is a view from the Fondamenta Sanudo looking north up the Rio della Panada towards the Calle Larga Giacinto Gallina bridge. I've got a map of Venice on the wall and I've stuck a pin in that place. There's no blue quite like the blue of water on a map – oceans and canals are equally profound in that blue.

I hadn't known Lavinia very long when I bought the picture. She'd invited me and a roomful of other people to dinner at her house in Battersea and we were looking at the work she'd hung around the place. My picture was on the wall that went up the stairs, not in a very good light. It's fairly small, twenty by twenty-five centimetres: in it are the shining murky water of the canal, some barges and mooring posts, some pink, brown, and ochreous houses with shadowy doorways, and one brown balcony overhanging the water; in the middle of the picture is the pinky-brown-ochre bridge with one or two figures crossing it. The right side of the picture is mostly in shadow, the left mostly in sunlight. The draftsmanship is not importunate: By the way, it seems to say, you might want to have a look at this if you've got a moment.

I've been to Venice just once, one weekend in 1945, some months before the end of the war. The famous bronze horses had been removed from the façade of the Basilica di San Marco for safety but I remember the winged golden lion on the clock tower, the blue and the gold and the metal statues of the Moors, how they pivoted from the waist as they struck the hours with their hammers, and the pigeons flying up in the piazza against the afternoon light that trumpeted even as it faded. I remember the slap and the hiss of the water along the sides of a gondola, the hauntingness of the light under bridges, the dancing waterlight and the shadow on canalside houses, the pleromatic depth and colour and luminosity of Venice: the light could almost be tasted like wine; the darks were juicy, musky, sweet, sombre, poignant, romantic, secret, tragic, dangerous, and always beckoning; wherever I looked my eye was drawn into the deeps of the ambient air that seemed alive and actively shaping the forms it defined.

I wanted my eye to be drawn into Lavinia's picture in the same way but it wasn't happening. I almost saw in it a little golden world of depth and light and air but it was as if between me and that world there was a membrane I couldn't break. I don't really want to pursue this metaphor but as far as I was concerned the picture was hanging on to its virginity. And all the while there was something about it that touched me: a modest but stubborn gallantry perhaps; it was what it was and it was true to that whatness, refusing to yield itself up to the casual viewer at first glance. Odd, I thought, to look so wild and free (which she always did) and paint so reticent a view.

Lavinia didn't miss much. 'I didn't mean to make you work so hard,' she said.

'Your pictures have to be looked at closely.'

'You mean they don't jump out and grab you.'

'I can't really say anything yet, I haven't looked long enough.'

'Looking longer may not help – they don't ask everybody in.'

Not perhaps the smoothest beginning for a friendship but we did become friends. I wanted the picture to ask me in, and when I got it home and saw it under a proper light it did, hospitably arranging its effects so that within the frame there appeared, in the colours and shapes and weights of forms and spaces, that little world of light and shadow that was Lavinia's Venice. Look, it said, look through here, beyond the bridge, all the way back – that little bit of pinky-golden light. See what I mean? I did see, and that picture and I have become very good friends. I used to find myself thinking about it often, the inwardness of it and the possibility that the painter, like the viewer, wanted something to open, wanted to be asked in.

Lavinia was (is?) tall and distinguished looking in a horsey long-faced Bloomsbury sort of way; she was much given to boots and cloaks and broad-brimmed hats and one wouldn't have been surprised to hear that she'd just come back from a solitary camel ride across the Empty Quarter. Where she'd actually come back from was always Venice, with a batch of paintings that she showed at an obscure gallery in Fulham which she left eventually because they never got her the prices she wanted and they never sold enough pictures.

She lived alone in a cluttered house that achieved a Venetian air on a very modest outlay: there were gilt things, rococo things, mirrors and candle sconces and hangings and of course her paintings. She acquired many of her household furnishings from skips and tips, kept (except for July and August and a week in November when I kept it) a black cat named Dis, complained constantly but not as if she meant it, and persisted gallantly with no recognition whatever. She lived on very little in Battersea and she lived on very little in Venice; she drove there in a grandmotherly blue Morris Traveller that was held together by false promises ('I swear I'll get you a new clutch in the spring') and the finely tuned harmonics of the noise it made; she managed to house-sit for absent Venetians whose houses commanded good views, she knew where to shop and she mostly ate in. She worked seven days a week and returned from her July-August stint with the Morris Traveller panting under yet more Santa Maria della Salutes seen from the Ponte dell'Accademia under serene or turbulent skies, Rio della Panadas caught in the changing lights of morning, afternoon, and evening, and many versions of an unnamed canal with barges in the foreground — she seemed dedicated to those three views.

Lavinia's letter continues:

... Did I say it was in November? Well it was, and
the mist was wet on our faces and the Grand Canal
was redolent of open and unknown seas. The mist was
like time made tangible – you could feel it on your face,
hold it in your hands, and have nothing. There are those
who accept the received world as the official version not
to be questioned but I find it highly questionable. I have
in my wallet a photocopy of a paragraph from a *Scientific American* article that I didn't see until two years
later:

> The many-worlds interpretation of quantum mechanics asserts there is no fundamental difference between
> the observed position of a particle and the other points
> to which the wave function assigned a non-zero probability. The particle exists at all the points. In order
> for this to be true, however, it is necessary to suppose there are infinitely many worlds, in each one
> of which the particle has a definite position. What
> happens during a measurement is that one world is
> selected from among the infinite range of possibilities.

We'd left the Accademia bridge, we were on a landing-stage feeling the mist on our faces and listening to foghorns
and the lapping of the water when I had the sensation of
the spinning, as big as the world, of an invisible wheel of
possibility in the mist. *Faites vos jeux – rien ne va plus*,
and a gondola slid out of the fourth dimension with a
shining wet blackness and operatic red cushions and a
fourth-dimensional gondolier at the oar. Did you know
that gondolas are asymmetrical? The right side is quite a
bit shorter and straighter than the left – I suppose this is
because the gondolier rows on the right and the shape of

the boat makes it easier to hold a straight course. If you think about it the whole thing becomes very metaphysical but then everything does.

We were in it then, listening to the slap and gurgle and hiss of the water along the sides until we were somewhere else and the gondola was gone and there was a blue neon sign, a glass door, and a very small reception desk where a massive sybilline red-haired woman surrounded by six or seven cats was smoking a little cigar and listening to *Tosca* on the radio. On the wall at the side of the desk was a signed photograph of Elvis Presley. *IL RE*, it said under the picture.

In the room the first thing I did was look out of the window. It was the hour *entre chien et loup*; in the canal below me a barge was moored, rocking a little as the water lapped and whispered in the twilight. It was a black barge with the waterline and the stern defined by red. Two white eye-discs on the bows with red many-pointed stars at their centres gave the barge an owl-faced look. On the glistening wet tawny canvas of the forward hatch sat a black cat looking up at me. A change came over the scene as if I were seeing it through a filter that deepened and intensified all the colour to many times its original strength. The air became a vibrant purple-blue that was so luminous, so bright, that it was the colour I'd use if I were painting lightning – the colour of the energy and the essence, the suddenly-here-and-now of lightning. I've often seen this colour behind my closed eyes but never before with them open. For the first time in my life the question itself became the answer. Ah, I thought, I *see*. I wanted to go on seeing like that but it lasted only a moment.

The hotel room, full of dusk and impermanence, seemed darker when I turned away from the window but we didn't switch on any lamps. There was dim blue wallpaper with faint golden stars. There were pink cyclamens in a glass vase on a table. On the wall was a framed reproduction of Guardi's *Partenza del Bucintoro il giorno dell'Ascensione*, which I thought very tactful of the management as all those cloaked figures in that little world selected for Guardi were watching the many-oared golden state barge and they had their backs to us. Downstairs *Tosca* was into Act Three, dawn was breaking over Rome, and Cavaradossi, with only minutes to live, was singing, '*Svanì per sempre il bel sogno d'amore . . .* '

> Vanished for ever the beautiful dream of love . . .
> The hour has fled,
> and I die without hope! . . .

We fell asleep to the sound of bells and foghorns. I'd taken the right side of the bed so that when I lay on my right side I was facing the window and away from him. When my eyes are closed I can always see better with the eye of the mind if I lie on my right side, and I wanted to get back to the heightened world of the purple-blue. My last thought as I fell asleep was: how am I going to manage that colour? Because it hadn't been stagey or artificial, it was simply a matter of being in that plane of being where that was how things looked. Giorgione, for all his mysticality, hadn't tried it in his lightning, if indeed that *was* meant to be lightning in *La Tempesta*. Had it been something between the barge cat and me or between him and me or was the barge cat inseparable from him and me and the purple-blue?

The next morning was a little like coming out of a cinema in the afternoon. It had been a marvellous night but now although the fog had gone the world seemed to have lapsed into owlish and blinking monochrome; everything was in the austere and dreamlike aquatint greys of Goya's *Los Caprichos*, so much so that I expected captions to appear in antique script beneath us: *El amor y la muerte*, something like that. Why? I had no idea. I'm a visual-minded sort of person and my mind lays on certain effects from time to time.

We had breakfast and I wanted to do a little work so I could see what kind of world would show up in my painting; I thought perhaps we could meet again in the evening. He said he had to see someone in Castello so I walked there with him, it wasn't far out of my way. He'd never been to Venice before, he'd told me he was here to research a first novel; we talked about books and pictures, that sort of thing, while crossing grey bridges under a grey sky and passing blind and blackened statues. We walked on grey paving stones pocked and pitted with time and history and worn by the footsteps of people walking into and out of the marvellous and the ordinary. At the Fondamenta Sanudo by the Rio della Panada, the place where I painted the picture you bought, he took out his pocket diary, consulted it, said he'd be back in fifteen minutes, and asked me to wait for him.

As he disappeared into the Calle Castelli I saw a photograph lying on the ground and I picked it up. There he was in living colour with his wife and children, two girls and a boy. He hadn't said he was married but then I hadn't asked him, had I. What had I expected at the age of forty-two – love's young dream? No, but really he oughtn't to have brought in Jeremiah and the storks over the Bosporus if all he wanted was a little action.

I stood by the statue of the Virgin while a wild-eyed woman in black came with breadcrumbs and fed a rabble of cynical-looking pigeons. '*Ecco!*' she said to them, '*Faites vos jeux – rien ne va plus.*' A Japanese family gave me their camera and smiled and I took pictures of them. Then I walked home and got my box-easel and went back to the hotel hoping for the barge and the black cat but they'd gone.

I've been back to Venice every year for two months
of bread-and-butter painting in July and August and
one week in November looking for the world of the
purple-blue. I've tried many times to do it from memory
but it won't come. I'd really like to see things that way
again. Today is the tenth anniversary of the day I met
him and I'll do what I always do, set up my box-easel
on the Ponte dell'Accademia or by the hotel (I call it the
Senza Nome, I never say or write its name) or on the
Fondamenta Sanudo where we parted. So far, although
I've seen and painted many worlds, I haven't yet found
the one with that owl-faced black barge on which the
black cat sat and looked up at me. It's misty today and
perhaps there's something in the air, some revolving of
possibilities. I feel a little strange but then I always do.
Maybe I'll try the Fondamenta Sanudo again.

Wish me luck –

Love,

Lavinia

There was a quick little pen-and-ink black cat at the bottom
of the letter. With the box-easel and Lavinia's letter the priest
enclosed a note he'd found with them asking that the painting
on the easel be sent to me.

'But there was no painting,' his letter goes on to say.
'Venezia, after all, swarms with collectors. The paintbox
sat on the parapet but on its easel there was nothing. In
the paintbox was money for the postage, so having nothing
else to send I send the box. The money was more than was
needed and the balance is enclosed. I emptied the palette cups
and I thought of cleaning the palette and the brushes but then
I thought it better not to do that.'

Some of the less-used colours she'd laid out round the
palette were crusted on top but still wet underneath. The
dried-up colours she'd been mixing were strange and wild

and other-worldly; among them and on one of the small bristle brushes was a very light bright purple-blue that I too have seen behind my closed eyes.

Good luck, Lavinia. If you're not with us any more I'll drink to my absent friend. But if you can read this where you are, maybe you'll think about coming home. They love you in Cork Street.

Dream Woman

The dim light, the faceful shadows murmured, tinkled, gleamed. The steady flame of the candle on the table made a globe of stillness around the two of us, a warm bright globe of stillness in which she raised her glass and the luminous rosy wine made a smaller bright globe, a little world of the poised wine of this moment. She tilted the glass, the wine poured out, its brightness in the candlelight falling, falling. With an indescribable smile she looked at me and poured out the wine and never said a word, saying with her smile that she knew herself to be a dream and lost to me. That was how the first time ended.

The next time I saw her she said straightaway, 'Why do you bother when you know I'm not real?'

'I don't know that. I refuse to know that.'

'How am I real then? You know I'm only a dream.'

'What is that? What does it mean when you say "only a dream"?'

'I'm only in your mind,' she said.

'What does that mean? The whole universe is only in the mind of God and nobody says the universe isn't real.'

'Maybe your mind isn't as real as God's mind. In any case you'll have to go back, you can't stay here. Why should I begin something with a man who can't stay?'

'You're in the world that's in me,' I said. 'I'll find

a way to stay.'

'For me there's no future in this. I've seen it happen before with dream women and realies and it never works.'

'Is that what they call us? "Realies"?'

'Yes, and it never lasts. They see the man a few times and that's the end of it. Sometimes they're left with a child. It's hardest on the children I think – it's like growing up in a whorehouse.'

'But you're not a whore. You're not here for anyone else, are you?'

'"Not here for anyone else"! You amaze me. I've seen you once before and for all I know I'll never see you again and you want me to keep myself pure for you. You're not even young: in a few years you'll be dead and this world in your head will still be here in other heads and I'll still be in it. What am I to do then, wear black and live on memories?'

'You're saying you've been with other men,' I said.

'Other realies.'

'You don't seem to have a very quick mind. How do you suppose I occupied myself until you turned up? With needlepoint? How would you like to live in this awful tatty place where nothing ever works properly? You go to the bathroom to wash your hair and maybe there's a sink and maybe it's the front half of a crocodile. Whole neighbourhoods disappear overnight without a trace, you're lucky if you can find the supermarket two days running. And in between times you sit around waiting like those whores in that painting by Toulouse-Lautrec. Sitting in that awful lounge in their depressing underwear and waiting for the punters.'

'Don't let's quarrel. It's only our second time together and I don't even know your name.'

'That's a typical realie remark. There aren't all that many names to be had for the asking around here, it isn't that pimple.'

'Surely you mean simple,' I said.

'Squeeze it how you like,' she said, and wasn't there any more.

Between then and the next time it occurred to me that perhaps if I could die while I was with her we might stay together always, moving from head to head as necessary.

The third time was in the same restaurant where she and I had sat together the first time. She was with Phil Worril. At school we used to call him Worril the squirrel. Her back was to me and Worril sat facing me in that same warm bright globe of candlelit stillness that had enclosed her and me. As I stood outside and looked past the menu in the window I saw his lips move but I couldn't make out what he was saying. She lifted her glass, luminous and rosy, bright globe of the poised wine of this moment, then she poured out its brightness in the candlelight.

I haven't seen her since. Sometimes when I'm doing the shopping I remember how she couldn't always find the supermarket.

Dark Oliver

Oliver sometimes dreamed a face that was green like pale fire, black like earth and ashes. It was huge, this face, and it was all around him as if it were the inside of an endless tube that slowly turned as he fell endlessly through it. And a sadness, an ache in the throat, a loss. What name was there to call? Who was gone? Oliver was ten.

The playground at school was for Oliver a grey place of rage and boy-sweat and Geoffrey. Geoffrey was two years older and four inches taller and he twisted Oliver's arm and rubbed his head in painful ways. Oliver fought him and lost. Geoffrey called him 'Olive Oil'. Geoffrey sang:

> 'Olive Oil had a boil
> right on the bottom of his bum.'

At the end of the summer term Oliver and his mother and father flew to Corfu and there they boarded a boat for the island of Paxos where they'd rented a house. The name in Greek letters on the bows of the boat was PERSEPHONEIA.

The air was clear, the sun was hot, the engine droned, the sunlight danced in dazzling points on the blue sea. There were stone fortresses, the coast was mountainous, on the upper deck a man played a bouzouki. The boat was full of people eating, drinking, smoking, playing cards.

Sun-glints moved slowly across the glasses and the bottles of beer and cloudy lemonade on the bar. On the lower deck were a lorry and two cars and a motorcycle; there were a goat and a donkey; there was a cockerel with bronzey and green and red feathers, it looked at the mountains and crowed. Oliver's father stood in the bow and looked down at the constant parting of the water that slid along the sides and joined the white wake marbling astern. His mother, her bare legs and sandalled feet already brown from afternoons at the Hurlingham Club, sat on a hatch cover, reading and smoking.

Oliver was listening past the drone of the engine, the slap of the bow wave, the jangling of the bouzouki: he was listening to the silvery flicker of olive trees in the sunlight, the olive trees of the island. It took so long to get there, hours and hours over the sea to the island.

When the boat dropped anchor in the harbour at Gaios and the chain rattled through the hawsepipe Oliver looked up at the hills and terraces beyond the red-tiled roofs of the town. 'What kind of trees are those?' he said. 'The silvery ones.'

'Those are olive trees,' said his mother.

'Persephoneia,' whispered Oliver.

'What are you whispering?'

'Nothing.'

The house looked as if it had been stained long ago with the juice of pomegranates. It had a red pantiled roof, it had a flagged courtyard. There was a table under a grape arbour; there were orange trees and a pomegranate tree. Oliver was astonished at the pomegranates, that this fruit he had read about in fairy tales should actually be growing on a tree where he was. He'd eaten pomegranate seeds at home but now as he held the fruit in his hand it was an orangey-red world of unknownness.

Oliver's father cut a pomegranate into thirds and offered

one to Oliver's mother. She looked at him as she bit into it but said nothing. For a moment the other two thirds lay on the white plate among drops of red juice. From a distance came the gigantic braying of a donkey, to Oliver it was the sound of something shut out and banished from happiness: it was a black sound that lay on the white plate with the two thirds of pomegranate and the drops of red juice.

'Persephone', said Oliver, 'ate seven pomegranate seeds in the realm of the dead and because of that she has to spend three months of every year down there with Hades and the earth is barren until she returns.'

'How many seeds have you eaten?' said his father to his mother.

'Too many,' she said.

Years later Oliver remembered some details and forgot others. He remembered tins of NOYNOY evaporated milk, they had a label with a picture of a pretty young Dutch woman breast-feeding a child, in the background a canal and windmills; he remembered bottles of gin with unknown labels, unremembered names; pistachio nuts; black wrinkled olives and goat cheese; mosquito-averting spirals of some green compressed substance that burned with the dark holiday smell of lost childhood.

He remembered a tiny dead scorpion on the floor of a cupboard. He remembered a polychaete sea-worm; magnified by the clear water, it was mythical-looking, pink and purple, its body fringed with undulating black bristles that moved it over the pale stones; the idea of it was huge.

There were three Swedish girls who wore no tops, their breasts were large and buoyant; they swam together like a sign of the zodiac.

One day a young woman in a black wet-suit speared an octopus. She slid it off the spear, took it by a couple of its arms and beat it to death on a flat rock, spattering Oliver with briny drops. Each time the octopus struck the rock it gripped it with its free arms, they came away with a sound like kisses.

Oliver and his mother went to the beach every day, his father less often. Oliver's mother swam, sun-bathed, smoked, wrote letters, read mysteries while his father sat at the table under the grape arbour, reading Marlowe's *Doctor Faustus* and making notes for his next book. In the evenings the two of them drank gin by candlelight.

Every day the sunshine was as flat as a postcard. Old women in black sat knitting outside the shops. At the harbour wall the old boatmen looked up from their boats as the near-naked summer women passed by.

Water for the house came from a cistern that was a little square edifice the same colour as the house, with steps going up to the low flat top of it. Rainwater supplied the cistern through a long pipe from the roof gutters of the house. Whenever a tap was turned on or the toilet flushed, the pump in the cistern gasped and panted as it laboured to bring water to where it was wanted.

Lying in his bed at night Oliver heard the crowing of a cock while the pump howled in the dark. He remembered the condemned voice of the donkey, the red juice of the pomegranate, the green and black face of his dream. At night this month of August was like a great animal of unknown shape and colour that turned and turned and turned away.

There were dry stone walls all over the island; they held the earthen terraces to the hillsides; sometimes they encircled single olive trees. Everywhere were stones and fragments of stone with flat surfaces that were good to draw on with a fibre-tip pen. Some were sand-coloured, some grey, some white. Some looked like curtains of stone, some like broken monuments. On the beach and in the water crouched great humped and hollowed ancient sea-worn shapes of stone. They had heard radios playing rock-and-roll and they had heard Orpheus. Lying half-submerged, Oliver held on to them while his body rose and fell with the rocking of the tide. Sometimes he spent hours on the beach bent over his shadow as he gathered hand-sized stones of various rounded shapes. Some of them fitted together in curious ways.

At first Oliver drew monsters and dragons on some of the stones; later he began to write on them. On some of the long-shaped rounded ones he wrote a single word in spirals round and round the stone: Down down down down down down .., or Groen green green green ... He also wrote, in the Greek letters he had seen on the boat, the name Persephoneia.

The road that led from the hills down into the town passed between terraces of olive groves. There was rubbish scattered everywhere, people simply threw it down the hillsides. Blue plastic mineral-water bottles were scattered through the olive groves where thrown-away cookers lay rusting. Many of the trees had been planted long, long ago when there were no such things as plastic mineral-water bottles. They twisted their roots into the stony ground of their stone-walled ter-races while in their silvery leaves the changing winds, the light of centuries whispered.

There was one particular olive tree that Oliver looked at whenever he passed it. Often there was a black donkey tied to it; sometimes there was a black-and-white goat nearby. The donkey was the one that Oliver had heard while eating the pomegranate under the grape arbour. When it opened wide its jaws and brayed it made a tremendous heehaw that was much too big a sound for an animal of that size; clearly the donkey was a medium for something else. This is my annunciation, said the voice that spoke through the donkey; this is my revelation of something so horrendous that there is no word for it and the voice with which I speak is taken no notice of.

67

The tree wasn't far from the house; Oliver went to it alone one afternoon. The donkey had wound its rope round and round the tree and now stood silent. The goat looked calmly at Oliver with its strange eyes that were like ochre-grey stones in which were set oblongs of black stone. A cock crowed among the blue plastic mineral-water bottles.

The tree was alive, there were silver leaves whispering in the sunlight, there were black olives growing on it. Yet the trunk was empty, it was only the shell of a tree with darkness inside the ancient twisted shape of it. The thick greenish-grey bark all ridged and wrinkled stood open as if two hands had parted it. The tree wasn't shaped like a woman and yet it was a woman-shaped tree, as if a woman had been wearing the tree and had stepped out of it.

Where is she now? thought Oliver. He looked at the ears of the donkey. What were they listening for? He looked at the eyes of the goat. What did they see that was different from what he saw? The cock crowed again.

'Here?' said Oliver.

The leaves whispered.

'Gone?' said Oliver.

The empty tree held open its darkness to him. The donkey sounded its tremendous heehaw, the goat looked at Oliver, the cock crowed a third time. Oliver stepped closer to the tree. He thought he heard music but he couldn't have said how it sounded. Perhaps it was only the idea of music in his mind.

Oliver was inside the tree, he didn't know how he'd got there. For a moment he saw the stone walls and the olive trees across the road, blue sky and silver leaves, green shade and golden sunlight and a yellow plastic meat grinder lying by the roadside; then everything blurred upward past him, he was falling, falling with a sick feeling in his stomach. There was a great sighing in him and around him; he remembered the eyes of the goat, the ears of the donkey.

Falling, falling, with the darkness leaping inside him like

a black frog, Oliver began to cry but it wasn't from fright, he was crying from sadness. With a terrible ache in his throat he was crying for something lost to him, he didn't know what. And all the time he was falling and wondering when he'd be smashed like an egg dropped from the nest.

A name was roaring in him, bellowing in him: PERSE-PHONEIA. He thought his skull would burst from it, he thought his bones would break from it. He was still fall-ing, he was nowhere, there was nothing but blackness, and into the blackness there came the idea of the face that he sometimes saw in his dreams Was he thinking it or was it thinking him? Inexplicably it was all around him as he fell. Bigger and bigger it grew, blotches of black on pale green, like a rubbing done on green paper. But the green was more like pale cold fire. Cold, yes, it was bitter cold, icy cold and a freezing wind blowing.

Oliver began to know that this was the face of Hades all around him; there was no end to it, the stony black and cold green fire of it turning, turning, a turning hollowness going straight down. Oliver fell and fell and kept on falling through it while the lips of Hades slowly moved, his mouth roared silently, PERSEPHONEIA.

Like the sea flooding a cave the idea of Hades and Persephone filled Oliver. It was in him that the green and golden summer of the world was winter for Hades, his black time, dead time, lost and broken time without Persephone. Persephone was everything beautiful and she was gone into the upper world of sunlight whispering in the olive groves. How could Hades know that she would ever come back to him? Why should she want to return to the sombre world of the dead as his dark queen? The king of the dead raged and wept in his terror, always turning, turning, slowly turning the face of his rage below the world.

Still Oliver was falling, and still that slowly turning face rushed upward from below all around him as he fell. The idea of it was too hard and heavy for him to hold in his mind, the pain of it was too much for him to bear. 'I think I'm going to die of it,' he said. But he didn't die.

The falling had stopped, the slowly turning face of Hades was gone. Oliver saw the eyes of the goat, he saw the donkey's ears turned back and listening. He heard the crowing of the cock, the whisper of the olive leaves. He was in the greenlit shade of the olive grove. The woman-shaped tree stood before him holding open its emptiness to him. Perhaps nothing had happened?

There was a stone in Oliver's hand that filled it comfortably and had a pleasing heaviness. It was a tawny broken stone with sharp edges and irregular facets that tapered to a triangular base; it looked like abstract sculpture of monumental size, it looked commemorative. There was a shallow concavity where his thumb fitted, and when he removed his thumb and held the stone at a certain angle to the light this hollow filled with the shadow of a great bird of the realm of the dead that stood with its back to him. He knew that it was a bird of power: it was a bird of loss, a winged sorrow for what was gone for ever. The thought of it was suddenly overwhelming and he cried.

Oliver thought of the stone as his Hades stone. He kept it in his pocket during the day and he kept it under his pillow at night. He didn't write on it or draw on it; with his thumb he felt the shape of the shadow-bird. He imagined it spreading its dark wings and he wondered about the unseen face of it.

When Oliver and his mother and father came back from Paxos the London streets looked mean and grey.

'Hades,' whispered Oliver.

'"Hell hath no limits,"' said his father, '"nor is circumscribed in one self place; for where we are is hell, and where hell is there must we ever be."'

'Speak for yourself,' said Oliver's mother.

*

When Oliver went back to school he had the Hades stone in his pocket, fitting his fingers, fitting his thumb.

It was a cold September, the air was grey, the streets were grey, the tarmac of the playground was hard under Oliver's feet.

There was Geoffrey again. 'Hello, Olive Oil,' he said.

Oliver didn't say anything. He saw the olive tree holding open its dark emptiness; with his thumb he felt the shape of the shadow-bird whose face he had not yet seen.

'What's the matter?' said Geoffrey. 'Cat got your tongue?'

Oliver took the stone out of his pocket. 'Do you know where this is from?'

'No. Where's it from?'

'Perhaps you'll find out soon. Hell hasn't got any limits – did you know that? It's wherever we are.'

'I think you've gone right round the twist, Olive Oil.'

'Perhaps you'll go somewhere too.' Oliver wanted to exact something from Geoffrey, wanted Geoffrey to feel the sorrow that he felt without knowing why. 'There's a darkness inside the tree,' he said.

'Sounds like there's a darkness inside your head.'

'Nothing is for ever – summer comes, summer goes. Geoffrey comes . . . '

'But he's jolly well not going, Olive Oil.'

Oliver moved back three steps. He tilted his head, listening to the great voice that spoke through the donkey. 'The darkness is waiting; the donkey says go.'

'You're the donkey and I think what you need is a good thumping.'

Oliver moved three steps to the left. He made his eyes like ochre-grey stones with oblong black stones set in them. 'The goat says go.'

'Baaa,' said Geoffrey. 'Why don't you try to make me go?'

Oliver moved forward three steps. At the back of his throat he crowed silently. 'The cock says go. Because it's time.'

'It's past time, Olive Oil,' said Geoffrey. He drew back his fist.

Oliver held the Hades stone so that the great shadowy bird appeared. He saw the bird rise high into the air, he saw its face that was black like earth and ashes, green like pale fire. 'Time for you to go,' he said to Geoffrey as the shadow bird stooped.

Oliver was all alone, falling endlessly while the slowly turning face of Hades rushed upward all around him. Not endlessly – he had stopped falling and it was the unturning face of the school nurse that he saw as he came awake gasping from the little bottle she held under his nose. The Hades stone was no longer in his hand.

'Are you with us again?' said the nurse.

'What happened?'

'It seems that you fainted after your exertions.'

'What exertions?'

'Geoffrey says you were showing him a judo throw.'

'Where's Geoffrey now?'

'They've taken him to hospital for stitches on his head. The playground is not the place for judo practice. Someone might have been seriously hurt.'

'We won't do it again.'

'I should hope not.'

'Here's your stone back,' said Geoffrey later. 'You know, it's a funny thing. When you bashed me with it I saw a great big face all around me, it was green and black and it kept turning.'

'I've seen that face,' said Oliver.

'Where? When?'

'On the island of Paxos last month.'

'How come you saw it?'

'I can't talk about it.'

'I'll swap you an Iron Maiden cassette for that stone.'

'Sorry, but no.'

'It's got my blood on it.'

'I've got another good stone from Paxos, from the beach; I'll give you that one but you have to stop calling me Olive Oil.'

'OK.'

The autumn term went well for Oliver; the other boys seemed to look at him differently from the way they had before. There was a school play about King Arthur and he was given the part of Merlin.

The Ghost Horse of
Genghis Khan

John was eight years old and he liked to be in his father's study. It was full of books and all kinds of things that his father needed for his writing. Sometimes after school John would lie on the oriental carpet and draw. Sometimes he would sit in the reading chair and read or look at videotapes that he listened to with headphones while his father worked.

There were shadowy places and lamplit places in the study. There were maps on the wall. There was a human skeleton that made gentle clacking sounds when you moved it. There were three pendulum clocks that struck the hours at different times when they were running. Now they were stopped at different times. There was a model of a Portuguese fishing boat, there was a stuffed barn owl. There were rocks and seashells from many places and a stone from a Crusader fort in Galilee with chisel marks on it. John ran his thumb over the chisel marks and thought of the hand that had held the chisel long ago. He held the left hand of the skeleton and moved its arm.

Among the clutter on the desk were some books with markers in them: *The Mongol Empire*; *The Mongols*; *The Devil's Horsemen*; *The Secret History of the Mongols*. John read bits here and there about Genghis Khan. He looked at drawings of thirteenth-century Mongol horsemen twisting in the saddle to shoot arrows. He read how Mongol children learned to ride before they could walk, how the warriors slept on horseback, how they drank the milk of their mares or opened a vein in a horse's leg to drink the blood.

'Genghis Khan,' he said aloud. He was alone in the lamplight and the shadows of the study. His father was in hospital, recovering from heart surgery. He slept wired to a cardiac monitor, his heartbeat regularly repeating its line of jagged peaks across the screen.

Genghis Khan, said John's mind. The mind was much older than the boy, it was as ancient as the stars, it remembered all sorts of things that John had never known. It was curious about everything and it was playful, it was obsessed with names and the sounds of words: Khwarizm; Khurasan; Karakorum; Genghis Khan. Genghis, Genghis, Genghis, it said, Genghis galloping, galloping. The thudding of unshod hooves is in the name; the bending of the bow is in the name, the bow of horn and sinew and lacquer. The rider twisting in the saddle draws the bowstring back and looses the arrow, the hiss of the hungry arrow cleaving time and darkness, cleaving forgetfulness so that the galloping of the ghost horse of Genghis Khan is fresh and strong in me.

The Mongols lived in tents, in yurts, thought John. My father and I have never slept in a tent. He sits at his desk writing except when he's napping or watching TV. He goes up and down the stairs slowly. I wonder what he was like when he was young. Did he ever gallop, did he ever have a bow and arrows?

In his father's typewriter was an unfinished page two. On the copyholder beside the typewriter was page one. It was headed: THE GHOST HORSE OF GENGHIS KHAN. John read:

Genghis Khan, the name lives its own life apart from the man who was whatever he was. Genghis, Genghis, Genghis Khan galloping, galloping in the long night. Hundreds of horses he must have ridden in his warrior lifetime and now he lies no one knows where and all the hundreds of horses have become one shape of galloping in the long night.

What colour is this galloping?

Red.

Is there a particular red horse?

There is now: a red roan with a white nose.

Is there a story about him?

Yes, I see it happening.

What do you see?

Here is Genghis Khan before he was Genghis Khan, when he was young, when he was called Temujin. Here he is, galloping for his life on the red roan. A close-coupled leggy horse, a clever-looking horse, a steadfast one, galloping, galloping. Behind him on the tawny steppe drifts the dust cloud of his going and through the dust gallop three riders hot on his track. Temujin has an arrow in his right shoulder, he cannot use his bow, nothing can save him but his horse. He leans low over its neck, he sees its eye roll back as the red roan listens for his voice.

'O thou of two worlds,' says Temujin. He doesn't know why he says this, he thinks of nothing, the words alone fill his mind, the surging gallop of the red roan is like a prayer wheel. On and on it gallops through the long afternoon, on and on until a long, long shudder . . .

There the unfinished page two ended. What do you think? said John's mind.

About what? said John.

About what's happening in the story, said his mind.

I'd rather not say, said John.

Three o'clock in the morning, said the three stopped clocks.

John looked at his watch. That isn't the time, he said. It's not even eight o'clock at night, it's not even my bedtime.

Not even your bedtime, said the clocks. Not all that much time though.

For what? said John.

It isn't for us to say, said the clocks.

John pushed the typewriter carriage return and the unfinished page moved up two spaces. That's not the end of the story, said his mind.

'Time to get ready for bed,' said his mother, and John went upstairs. His mother kissed him good night and he fell asleep and his mind began to speak to him again.

What is the shape of the galloping of the ghost horse of Genghis Khan? it said. Not of the eye, not to be seen, shadow of a memory, hoofbeats on the plains of here and gone. Here and gone, thought John in his sleep. Two places. Is there a drum, said his mind, is there a rattle, is there a bone whistle? How does one call up the ghost horse of Genghis Khan? Out of the herds of the dead, out of the shadows and the dust and the silence, out of the white pages of scholars and the smell of ink how does one call up that moving shadow on the screen of memory?

If you call me I will come, said the ghost horse.

Where are you? said John.

In your mind, said the ghost horse. In the shadows and the long night and the herds of the dead.

I don't know your name, said John. How can I call you if I don't know your name?

My name is not a name, said the ghost horse. Call me how you can. Call me and I will come.

What is it to be alive? said the sleeping John. What is it to be dead?

Ideas never die, said the ghost horse. I am an idea.

John woke up and went into his father's study. He turned on the lamps so that the places of lamplight and shadow appeared in their proper order. Three o'clock in the morning, said the three stopped clocks.

John looked at his watch. That's not the time, he said. It's only a little past two. Only a little past two, said the clocks. John looked at them very hard. They were telling the right time. He wound them and started them going. Then he sat down at the typewriter.

The unfinished page seemed to move in its blank whiteness, seemed to dance in its blankness before him. In that dancing was the red roan galloping, galloping until a long, long shudder broke its rhythm. In everything, said his mind, there is the animal of itself, the animal beyond the moment, beyond all moments. In the horse and in the man and in the boy, the animal of itself galloping, galloping.

John felt the dancing in the paper move towards him as he moved towards it. I'm not as good at stories as my father is, he said.

It isn't a question of being good at stories, said his mind. It's a question of how far you'll go.

At three o'clock in the morning in the hospital ward the pattern on the cardiac monitor lost its regularity and jumbled into random peaks and valleys. The staff nurse flung the pillows off John's father's bed and began to massage his chest while a student nurse gave him mouth-to-mouth respiration. The night sister dialled 222, said, 'Cardiac arrest!' and ran for the emergency trolley. 'Crash!' said the bleepers as the student started a bicarbonate drip while the staff nurse put an airway into John's father's throat and attached a re-breather bag. When the crash team arrived the anaesthetist inserted an endotracheal tube, put John's father on oxygen, and took over the re-breather. The doctor at the defibrillator applied the electrode jelly and said, 'Stand back.' He pressed the paddles against John's father's chest and delivered a 400-joule shock; John's father arched convulsively but the random peaks and valleys continued on the monitor screen. 'Stand back,' said the doctor, and did it again.

What did you say? said John to his mind.

I said it's a question of how far you'll go.

John wasn't aware of answering but he must have said

something, thought something. There was a horrendous rushing, ripping, rending sound, a searing blast of pain as all before and after tore away from him and all the clocks struck three.

He whirled through blackness, wheeled high up into clear blue air and scanned the tawny steppe below him, saw the dry dust drifting, saw the horses and their riders strung out on the lion-coloured plain. Their shadows raced in silence over pebbles, blades of grass, old hoofprints. In the distance stood the wrinkled silent mountains, intolerably real.

Then the ground swooped close and blurred back under him in utter silence, he was in the galloping, in the animal of it. On and on he galloped; an immense fatigue dragged at him and there came a long, long shudder but the animal of him left all else behind, the animal of him became its motion, became the never-tiring motion of itself as sounds rushed in upon him, the incessant rhythmic thudding of his galloping hooves. He felt the weight of his rider, felt his own unending strength become a long, long rocking like the sea and far away.

In the hospital his father opened his eyes. 'O thou of two worlds,' he said.

'How are you feeling?' said the night sister.

'I almost didn't get here.'

'Tell me about it.'

'I felt my horse sink underneath me, then . . . '

'Then what?'

John's father laughed. 'It was a dream,' he said.

It was almost four o'clock in the morning when John's mother woke up and went into the study. She saw her son asleep at the desk with his head cradled on his arms. She read the page in the typewriter that had ended: ' . . . on and on until a long, long shudder . . . ' Now there was more. She read:

79

. . . on and on until a long, long shudder passes through the horse but it doesn't stumble, it keeps on galloping. The pursuers have no more arrows and they stop chasing Temujin.

It was getting dark when the red roan brought Temujin to his camp. His brother Khasar pulled out the arrow and bandaged the wound and got him a fresh horse. It was time to move camp, and they rode away. Temujin's wound hurt, he'd lost a lot of blood. He fell asleep in the saddle.

When he woke up the moon was shining and they were up in the hills. The horses were put out to graze and he went to look for the red roan but he couldn't find it.

'Where's the red roan?' he asked Khasar.

'How should I know?' said Khasar.

'But I rode into camp on it,' said Temujin.

'I found you lying on the ground at the edge of camp and there was no horse,' said Khasar.

'Were there any tracks?'

'No tracks.'

Then Temujin knew that the red roan had galloped beyond death to save him.

In two weeks John's father came home. He sat down at his desk and looked at the page in his typewriter. 'Someone's been typing on my page,' he said.

'It was me,' said John. 'I woke up in the middle of the night and came in here and I sort of had a dream at your desk.'

'Sleeptyping?' said his father.

'Something like that,' said John.

'It's not bad,' said his father. 'Not bad at all.'

A LIBRETTO

Some Episodes in the History of Miranda and Caliban

An entertainment in two acts with music by Helen Roe

The way I see it Shakespeare didn't invent Caliban; Caliban invented Shakespeare (and Sigmund Freud and one or two others). Caliban is one of the hungry ideas, he's always looking for someone to word him into being so he can have another go and maybe win Miranda this time or next time. Caliban is a necessary idea. I can imagine The Tempest *without Ferdinand but not without Caliban.*

CHARACTERS

Miranda and all other female characters   *mezzo-soprano*
Caliban and all other male characters   *baritone*
Narrator

There are no costumes, no props, and no sets. The narrator will sit at one side of the stage. Miranda and Caliban will either stand or sit as convenient and when necessary will minimally indicate the action.

Act One

NARRATOR Machine-gun fire, heavy artillery. Caliban and Miranda crossing a vast and meaningless desolation with shells bursting all around them.

MIRANDA Which way is the sea?

CALIBAN I don't know.

MIRANDA How far is it?

CALIBAN I don't know.

MIRANDA Caliban, *is* there a sea?

CALIBAN There is a sea, I have it in my mind all small and perfect, like blue enamel on a snuffbox.

MIRANDA They're getting closer. I'll try to slow them down.

NARRATOR She runs off. Caliban takes cover in a shell-hole.

CALIBAN How in the world did it come to this? I think back over what's happened and I can't seem to get my mind around it.

NARRATOR Big explosion close by. Miranda appears with box stencilled: NANDICAL GLOBAL UNLIMITED – 50 BIG BANGERS.

CALIBAN What happened?

MIRANDA I raided an ammo dump, blew up a bridge. Let's not hang about.

NARRATOR Artillery continues as they move forward cautiously.

CALIBAN There is a blue enamel sea so far away, in it
the legs of Icarus are disappearing with a tiny
distant splash in utter silence . . .

MIRANDA . . . disappearing, no one hearing.

CALIBAN The legs of Icarus disappearing by some distant
    curving
shore where stands a white and shining city . . .

MIRANDA What a pity.

CALIBAN On the hill a ploughman dances in the furrow . . .

MIRANDA Perhaps his horse is singing.

CALIBAN And a shepherd looks up at the sky where
    Icarus no longer is.

MIRANDA Full fathom five my father lies;
in the place where myth has dropped him;
yearning still for farther skies,
wondering sometimes just what stopped him.
Still he hopes to fly again,
vows that he will try again,
thinks he might have done the thing
with a better sort of wing.

CALIBAN Icarus isn't your father.

MIRANDA Icarus is everybody's father.

CALIBAN How's that?

MIRANDA He fell.

CALIBAN Is this some doctrine of original fallibility or what?

MIRANDA Fathers fall. Look at Adam, and he wasn't even trying to fly.

CALIBAN Icarus falling, cleaving the high blue air in his long, long plunge to the slow and ceaseless changing of the waves far, far below.

MIRANDA Falling from his dream of flight he breaks the pictured surface to become the ancient green and sea-shapen strangeness of you.

CALIBAN Me!

MIRANDA Always Icarus tries to fly and always he falls, and as often as he falls you rise up from the vasty deeps . . .

CALIBAN . . . to let him become me, to take upon myself his failure and his fall and to sink back to the slow green depths with it . . .

MIRANDA . . . humble and great. Icarus has the courage to attempt his flight only because he knows that you are waiting below him.

NARRATOR They take cover as fighter planes pass overhead, strafing.

MIRANDA When Icarus becomes you, you become everybody's father.

CALIBAN Full fathom five your father lies;
like a flounder on the bottom . . .

MIRANDA The submerged father is changed into something rich and strange so that the daughter can re-encounter him as Caliban-Icarus.

CALIBAN That's deep.

MIRANDA Five fathoms.

NARRATOR Heavy shelling. They fling themselves down. Caliban is hit.

MIRANDA Caliban! You're hit!

CALIBAN Bit of shrapnel, I'll be all right. I don't remember Icarus becoming me.

MIRANDA It happens in a forgotten world that's always gone.

CALIBAN Did our story begin in that forgotten world?

MIRANDA We had no story there.

NARRATOR Battle sounds down, the light goes green and dim.

MIRANDA Deep of unknowing, deep of our yester, there
    we were
nameless, just what we were, we had no story, nothing to
part us, we had each other, we had our love.

NARRATOR Greener and dimmer, we see only uncertain shapes.

HE Small in the deep I am, strange to
myself, not knowing who I am, not knowing
what I am. Perhaps I'm the darkness,
the darkness itself.

SHE Strange like the sea you are, strange like
the darkness, strange like the sea-shapen
rocks of the shore.

BOTH Now we are one thing, we are the wild green, we
are the green sea that heaves its great back under
bird cry and wing-swoop and wind, we are the
great sea that booms in the spoutholes and crashes in

echoing caves of the shore. Now we are quiet,
now we are deep, deep, deep, deep.

HE I am the stranger, the dark one, the diver . . .

SHE . . . the shadow side of darkness and the night's
left hand.

HE And in this hand the stars I hold, the
sea, the white fog on the water, dark of
love, deep mirror of the mystery, you.

SHE Show me myself.

HE Sarabands you dance on golden sands . . .

SHE Sarabands I dance on golden sands,
and mystery, and chance, and in my hands
are golden moments, golden evenings by the sea
and golden moons, and we
two are each other, you and I,
one thing for ever.

HE We will always be each other.

SHE Out of unknowing will come the story of us and
our names.

HE I don't want to know our story and our names.

SHE Out of now will come the future, our unknowing will be lost and never found again and we shall
forget.

HE Must we forget?

SHE Life would be too sad if this dim
beauty could be remembered. Out in the world we
must forget this time, we must live out our . . .

HE . . . story that waits for us. I'm afraid I'll lose you.

SHE There will be times, times when we . . .

HE ... find each other? Will there be ... ?

SHE ... times when we find each other, and when ...

HE ... we find each other, you mustn't lose me ...

SHE ... you mustn't lose me, left hand of night, reach out ...

HE ... and take you, take you and hold you.

BOTH Don't let me go.
I won't let you go.

HE I'm holding you now.

SHE What's this?

HE What's what?

SHE This little thing I've got my hand on.

HE It's not me.

SHE Oh, dear, it's coming away in my hand.

NARRATOR A dreadful gurgling is heard as the Deep of Unknowing goes down the plughole. The greenness and the dimness drain out of the scene and we see Her dressed as William Shakespeare and sitting at a desk on which are a typewriter and a ream of yellow paper.

HE Who are you?

SHAKESPEARE Greatness has been thrust upon me, I feel such a pentametric urging, such a strong dramatic surging, such a vast cathartic purging that I scarcely can contain all the bulging of my brain: I have many things to do, one of which may well be you. My name is Shakespeare, William Shakespeare. Who are you?

HE I'd rather not say.

SHAKESPEARE Why not?

HE I'm afraid you'll write a play.

SHAKESPEARE But that's what I do.

HE That's what I was afraid of.

SHAKESPEARE I feel as if our fates are intermingled,
    I feel as if . . .
I became Shakespeare, Shakespeare to find
you, spotted and reeking, smelling of low-tide
sea-wrack and shipwreck, semen and sweat, loneliness,
madness, joy long departed, trouble unending, leafy and
shadowed forests of midnight, beaches of morning. I
became Shakespeare, Shakespeare to find you, keep in
my mind you, orphan and nameless, dark child and
doomful, on you impending annihilation . . .

HE Annihilation!

SHAKESPEARE On the wild dark of you, on the sweet
night of you, civilisation.

HE Why must I be civilised?

SHAKESPEARE That's how things are: the world will
take away the island of you and the sea, the shadow
of you and the silence, and then there will be no more
you.

HE And that's my story, is it?

SHAKESPEARE Quiet — from deep in the depths of my
brain a name is rising — a name full of the strangeness and
the darkness of you, the terror in you and the terrifyingness
of you. In that name are all the unseen changing colours and
the unknown music of you.

HE Here it comes, I can see it coming and I don't know
how to stop it.

SHAKESPEARE Punger, Ponger, Bonger, Slonger.

HE Too simple.

SHAKESPEARE Glimmerdim,   Gleamdeep,   Greenshadow,
Snelg.

HE Snelg isn't bad.

SHAKESPEARE Belziflung, Fliskerbung, Gungifer, Noog.

HE Noog?

SHAKESPEARE It wants more of a slanty something to it,
more of a cannibal, cabinal, banical sort of a sound.

HE What it wants is a chance to get out of this
story.

SHAKESPEARE Calical, Baniban, Caliban.

CALIBAN That's it, I'm done for.

SHAKESPEARE Caliban is who you are, Caliban is you.

CALIBAN Miranda!

NARRATOR Reaches for her with his left hand. She backs
away.

SHAKESPEARE/MIRANDA Who's Miranda?

CALIBAN You are. In the sound of my name I heard
yours. Don't write our story, stop now.

SHAKESPEARE/MIRANDA Miranda is admirable, she's *mirabile*,
she mirrors things, she's very beautiful.

NARRATOR Typing slowly and thoughtfully.

SHAKESPEARE/MIRANDA This awful-looking Caliban creature
loves her but she can never be his.

CALIBAN Awful-looking? Never be his?

SHAKESPEARE/MIRANDA Poor   old   ugly   Caliban's   living

alone on this island when the beautiful Miranda and her father fetch up here somehow, they're shipwrecked or marooned or whatever. The father has a very elegant tum-te-tum sort of name like Maximo, Paximo, Pompero, Properso . . .

CALIBAN Prospero.

SHAKESPEARE/MIRANDA A very scholarly man, deeply versed in the occult arts. He used to be a duke or something like that but he got slung out by some bad people. Prospero and Miranda were cast adrift in a little boat and that's how they got here.

NARRATOR Lightning and thunder.

CALIBAN I think we're going to have rain.

SHAKESPEARE/MIRANDA All the bad people are on a ship and Prospero magics up some heavy weather, a big storm, to bring them to the island. *Heavy Weather*, by William Shakespeare. No. *The Big Storm*, by William Shakespeare. No.

CALIBAN *The Tempest?*

SHAKESPEARE/MIRANDA *The Tempest*. Act One, Scene One. A tempestuous noise of thunder and lightning heard.

NARRATOR Thunder and lightning.

CALIBAN If it's about me why don't you simply call it *Caliban?*

SHAKESPEARE/MIRANDA Actually I've no idea what it's going to be about.

CALIBAN It's going to be about how you sail away and leave me, that's what. And only a few minutes ago you said that you became Shakespeare in order to find me. Do you remember that?

SHAKESPEARE/MIRANDA Find you as part of a gestalt is
what I meant – I was talking about Art. If it should come
to a sailing-away you must bear in mind that there's such a
thing as dramatic inevitability.
If I should have to break your heart,
that's how it is, my dear, with Art.
If I should have to sail away
and leave you, that's the price we pay.
It isn't easy being The Bard,
sometimes I find it bloody hard.

BOTH It isn't easy being The Bard,
sometimes one finds it bloody hard.

SHAKESPEARE/MIRANDA Though striving as per Aristotle,
one easily can lose one's bottle
and ruin things with mawkish error,
not purging pity nor yet terror:
we're talking Drama here, my friend –
there may not be a happy end.

BOTH It isn't easy being The Bard,
Sometimes one finds it bloody hard.

CALIBAN I think that Art is truly magic,
I wonder though, need it be tragic?
Might not true lovers stay together
however wild and rough the weather?
Might not the genius of The Bard,
deal you and me a better card?

BOTH It isn't easy being The Bard,
sometimes one finds it bloody hard.

SHAKESPEARE/MIRANDA Melpomene, the tragic muse,
sometimes comes in for much abuse
from those who want their jam today
and think there is no price to pay,
but though true Art may wound and irk us,

I offer neither bread nor circus.
Believe me, Caliban, old fruit,
I'll cry when I give you the boot.

BOTH It isn't easy being The Bard,
sometimes one finds it bloody hard.

CALIBAN When you become Shakespeare you really become Shakespeare.

SHAKESPEARE/MIRANDA Enter a Shipmaster and a Boatswain. (*She pronounces 'Boatswain' as spelled.*)

CALIBAN Bosun.

SHAKESPEARE/MIRANDA What's that?

CALIBAN You don't say 'Boatswain', you say 'Bosun'.

SHAKESPEARE/MIRANDA How do you know?

CALIBAN I don't know, it's a word I must have heard somewhere.

SHAKESPEARE/MIRANDA If Boatswain is Bosun then I suppose my name is Shaysper, is it?

CALIBAN I never said so.

SHAKESPEARE/MIRANDA Good. Enter a Shipmaster and a Boatswain. (*Pronouncing it as before.*)

CALIBAN I'm beginning to remember this time that never happened. I remember a grey misty morning and the sound of the boat's keel scraping the sand. Prospero didn't move, I thought he was dead. Miranda was such a little thing, all forlorn, and I thought of her in that leaky boat far out at sea; they'd have had to keep bailing all the time to stay afloat . . .
Far out at sea, and the waves like
mountains toppling under a black sky, far

out at sea where death hums its beckon, hums
its deep song on the wind, you in your frail boat,
Miranda. Oh, the pity of it! I am so afraid, Miranda,
when I think of how I might have lost you, might
never have seen you, never have known there
had ever been you, Miranda.
Soon Prospero was strong enough to sit up and order
me about. But Miranda was my friend, we fished and
swam together and drifted in the island silence in the long
afternoons.

NARRATOR *Picks up pages and reads.*

CALIBAN Boatswain, Antonio, Gonzalo, mm hmm. Prospero,
Miranda, Ariel. Boring, boring, boring. What's this?
Prospero says, 'We'll visit Caliban, my slave.' And Miranda
says, ''Tis a villain, sir, I do not love to look upon.' I,
a villain!

SHAKESPEARE/MIRANDA Read on, you'll see why she says
that.

CALIBAN Now Prospero says to me, 'Thou did'st seek to
violate the honour of my child.' Ah.

NARRATOR Caliban becomes Sigmund Freud from the waist
up. Shakespeare/Miranda becomes straight Miranda and lies
down on a couch.

FREUD/CALIBAN Can you tell me what happened?

MIRANDA They'd been swimming and they went out too
far. She grew tired and called to him. He brought her back,
his arm across her breasts as he pulled her in to shore. She
lay in the shallows in her shining nakedness and she kissed
him and would have given herself to him but Prospero came
and beat him and cursed him and put spells on him that made
him sick.

FREUD/CALIBAN
(*Aside*)
My pleasure is not unalloyed
in being Caliban and Freud.
Though deeply analytical
I'm somewhat hypocritical,
and rather beastly, I suppose
and savage underneath my clothes.
I'd like to have her here and now,
instead of which I smile and bow
and ask about her dreams.
(*To Miranda*)
Can you remember when these Calibantasies began?

MIRANDA I'd always wanted Caliban, always lusted after the sweet reek of him, the heat of him in the dark of love. Before I could find him I had to find the island he lived on; so I became Shakespeare and invented it.

FREUD/CALIBAN And Caliban appeared.

MIRANDA Prospero turned up first – you know, my dad.

FREUD/CALIBAN Or so he said.

MIRANDA What do you mean, 'Or so he said'?

FREUD/CALIBAN I mean who is Prospero?

MIRANDA I've told you, he's my dad.

FREUD/CALIBAN Nothing is that simple.
With love you can't take anything for granted
when dealing with a woman and a man;
emotion sometimes gets a little slanted –
could Prospero perhaps be Caliban?

MIRANDA What a load of Calibollocks.

FREUD/CALIBAN Did he love you like a father?

Did he father like a lover?
It's an awful lot of bother
and one seldom can discover
with a woman and a man,
just exactly when he's Prospero and
when he's Caliban.
Well, I mean you've got to look at this
in every way you can —
was your lover really Prospero
or was he Caliban?
Of course this leaves out Ferdinand entirely, but at
the deeper levels, you see, he simply doesn't come into
it.

MIRANDA How could Prospero be Caliban when they
both have to be onstage at the same time?

FREUD/CALIBAN Each occupies the psychological space
ostensibly left vacant by the other. But your Shakespearean
super-ego wouldn't accept either of him as a lover; hence
Ferdinand the dummy escort, the waxwork dressed up in a
Ferdinand suit.

MIRANDA Ferdinand is with Nandical Global Unlimited
now. He uses Big Bang aftershave, drives a red Porsche,
reads a pink newspaper, and comes to bed with a book
called *99 Possible Positions*.

FREUD/CALIBAN What sort of positions?

MIRANDA Financial. He was never my type but when I
became Shakespeare I had to write Shakespeare's *Tempest*.
And when I became Miranda I had to speak the lines that
Shakespeare wrote: one thing simply led to another; one
does what's expected of one, so at the end of the play I
sailed away.

NARRATOR She sails away, leaving the typescript behind.
Freud/Caliban is still taking notes.

97

FREUD/CALIBAN You sailed away. Miranda? MIRANDA! MIRANDA! Gone? O God, she's gone.

NARRATOR Looks at typescript.

FREUD/CALIBAN She sailed away and married Ferdinand and they jumped into bed and they did it and did it and did it. THEY DID IT ALL THE TIME, NIGHT AND DAY, SHE COULDN'T GET ENOUGH OF IT! Why didn't I strangle Ferdinand? All I had to do was put my two hands round his neck and squeeze a little. Prospero would've killed me for it but I'd have died in hot blood and good spirits. Too late. Miranda's gone and here I am. LEFT!

NARRATOR UnFreuds himself.

CALIBAN No more dressing up. I am alone, bereft, unaccompanied. This is my essential condition. A whole play was written with a ship, an ocean, an island, and twenty or thirty people, and as far as I can see its only purpose was to leave me here alone.

NARRATOR We hear rain and the sighing of the sea.

CALIBAN In the rain the sea is sighing as it brings and
brings again its long self to the strand, brings and
brings again its long self to the shore where
memory hangs like white fog drifting, white fog on
the water whispering regret, whispering the sadness of
what never happened; whispering the dimming of the
light, the salt-sea dusk where I loom huge and
strange, where I go very small. CAL-I-BAN!
Caliban, Calibonely,
oh so very green and lonely,
green and lonely, deep and mad
Caliban, Calibendous
In my huge and my tremendous, in my
slow gigantic changes like the sea, like the sand,
I'm the shadow side of darkness,

I'm the night's left hand.
Prospero took her away but he left his magic book behind.

NARRATOR Goes off. Splash. Comes back dripping wet with
Prospero's book.

CALIBAN What a liar you are, Prospero. You said you'd
drown it 'deeper than did ever plummet sound' and here it
was in only five fathoms of water. Is that all the deep you
are, old man?

NARRATOR Opens book. Lightning and thunder. Drops
book.

CALIBAN I'm sorry, I'm sorry, I won't do it again!

NARRATOR Distant thunder. Rain.

CALIBAN Ordinary thunder, ordinary rain.

NARRATOR Picks up book, scans pages.

CALIBAN Where are all those spells he used to write down?
The book is full of emptiness; he made his ink from berries
and the sea washed it away. Rotten empty book. Not that I
could read it now that I've gone primitive.
In the rain the sea is sighing as it brings and
brings again its long self to the shore where
memory hangs like white fog drifting, white fog on
the water whispering regret, whispering the sadness of
what never happened . . .
I can feel a power in these empty pages. Is it the power
of Prospero's regret? Are you sorry that you took Miranda
away from me? Will the power of your regret bring her back
to me?

NARRATOR Darkness comes.

CALIBAN Night and darkness, bring, bring, bring
Miranda to her Caliban, her dark one, green one, mad
one, sad one, bring her to her one and

only true love, yes, to me, Miranda,
Miranda to me, come, come, come!

NARRATOR A scream. Lights. Miranda in a nightie struggles with Caliban.

MIRANDA Get off me, you awful thing! Ugh! You smell all fishy and low-tide and seaweedy and you're all wet and cold and horrible. Stop it!

NARRATOR She knees Caliban.

CALIBAN Ooh, ooh! Ow! Miranda, it's me, Caliban!

MIRANDA Don't I know it! Who else could smell like that! I'm so glad this is a dream and now I'll wake up in bed with Ferdinand and you'll be gone.

CALIBAN It's not a dream, you're here with me on our island.

MIRANDA How'd I get here?

CALIBAN Prospero's book.

NARRATOR Thumping the book with her fist.

MIRANDA Take me home this instant!

NARRATOR Blackout.
(*When the lights come up Miranda's gone.*)

CALIBAN Maybe regret isn't strong enough.

INTERVAL

Act Two

NARRATOR Darkness. Caliban with Prospero's book.

CALIBAN By the power of Prospero's regret, by the power of my longing, let Miranda not be married to Ferdinand and let the past be wiped out. Put her where there's no Ferdinand and put me in the same place.

NARRATOR Lights. Miranda alone in a desert place.

MIRANDA A desert! Who am I? Why am I so full of longing and regret?

NARRATOR The Little Black Thought comes in.

L.B.T. Psst! The Little Black Thought am I. How do you doing?

MIRANDA Why do you talk that way?

L.B.T. Foreign to you I am, yes. Therefore foreignly I speak.

MIRANDA Little Black Thought, did you say?

L.B.T. Yes, that is what. You can call me L.B.T.

MIRANDA I don't think I want to call you anything.

L.B.T. I have a little something for you. Your attention, please.

NARRATOR Exposes knickers, on them the word DESPAIR.

L.B.T. Look on my works, Miranda, read.

MIRANDA Despair. I'm not interested.

L.B.T. That's all right, I'll be interested for both of us.

MIRANDA Suddenly you're not foreign.

NARRATOR Darkness as the Little Black Thought overpowers
Miranda.

L.B.T. Now I am on you, holding you tight,
Little Black Thought am I, claiming my right.
Feel me, Miranda, feel me inside you —
strongly I ride you, take you, possess you,
sweetly and soothingly now I caress you,
leaving within you my seed to depress you.
Beauty so fair, bear my despair.

NARRATOR Lights.

L.B.T. My seed has gone into you.

MIRANDA I noticed.

L.B.T. I do it in a rather special way.

MIRANDA Do you think so?

L.B.T. Tomorrow morning you'll give birth to my child.

NARRATOR Gives her a bag.

MIRANDA What's this for?

L.B.T. To put over your head.
When a black moon, yes, a black moon rises in a sky
    all bloody red,

when Dracula's alive and well and Goldilocks is dead,
when an icy wind is blowing through the petrified trees,
and your boggled mind is crawling on its boggled hands
    and knees,
when there's moaning down the chimney and you dial
    nine nine nine,
and a voice says, 'SIX SIX SIX HERE. WILL IT BE YOUR
    PLACE OR MINE?'
then you'll look up at that red sky and you'll tear out
    all your hair
'cause you're looking at that dreadful, dreadful CHILD OF
    DESPAIR,
and you're bald but that won't help you, and you know
    you're almost done . . .

MIRANDA It'll be quite large, will it?

L.B.T. Also ugly. But it won't hang about. As soon as
it's born it'll go looking for a mate. All you have to do
is . . .
. . . turn it loose and let it go, just let it run.
That's how it likes it, baby, that's how it's done.
You don't have to name it . . .

MIRANDA I don't have to claim it.

L.B.T. Turn it loose and stand aside and . . .

MIRANDA . . . just let it run.

L.B.T. Just let it run, baby, just let it run,
sometimes a really big despair can be a lot of fun,
let it have a little buzz, let it do the things it does,
you don't have to love it, baby . . .

MIRANDA . . . just let it run.

L.B.T. Day after tomorrow you'll be a grandmother
unless . . .

MIRANDA Unless what?

L.B.T. Unless you do it with someone else before cock-crow.

MIRANDA There don't seem to be a lot of cocks around here.

L.B.T. It's nothing you need to think about and you won't because now you're going to forget what I've just told you and everything else that's happened between us. Ta ra.

NARRATOR He's off.

MIRANDA In the Babylon of my anger, by the dry
river of memory, I wept but could not remember
the Zion of me, wept and hung my harp on
starlight and the dry wind. In the pleasant
palaces the wild dogs howl; I wait through
dawns and noonings, undulant and still like the
desert. I watch the distance shimmering on the
long sands and I dream a solitary traveller
approaching. What is he? What will he be to me?

NARRATOR She becomes a sphinx. Caliban enters as a traveller, doesn't see her.

TRAVELLER Probably this is a dream. Perhaps I sailed across a small and . . .

SPHINX . . . perfect blue enamel sea in which the legs of Icarus are disappearing with a tiny distant splash.

TRAVELLER In this dream the air is quick with danger, I smell lions and honey. Almost . . .

BOTH . . . I remember one who dances sarabands on golden sands . . .

NARRATOR He sees the sphinx.

TRAVELLER . . . almost I remember this one crouching lion-coloured and implacable. The dry wind and the desert sing around her. I think she is dreaming me.

BOTH Such a very real dream, so crystalline and clear, like a painting done by Dali or a peepshow in an alabaster egg.

SPHINX This seems a low-tide traveller; he smells of sea-wrack and shipwreck, semen, sweat, loneliness and madness, joy long departed and trouble unending; fear and lust and strangeness.

TRAVELLER She smells of lions and honey, of death and life. I'm afraid she'll kill me but I think of mounting her and biting her neck.

SPHINX That's a daring thing to say. Who are you?

TRAVELLER It's your dream – call me anything you like.

SPHINX I don't think dreams have smells like yours. Pinch me.

TRAVELLER O God.

SPHINX Do it.

NARRATOR He does it.

SPHINX I'm not dreaming. Pinch yourself.

NARRATOR Pinches self.

SPHINX You're not dreaming either. Now then, tell me your name.

TRAVELLER I don't remember.

SPHINX You can't be that deeply unknowing. Try.

TRAVELLER I feel a kind of not of the bravest poor-John.

SPHINX That's a low-spirited sort of name.

P. JOHN I'm a low-spirited sort of person just now.

SPHINX Is there something familiar about you? Was there a time when we were something else?

P. JOHN I don't know. You haven't told me your name.

SPHINX I live without a name, mysterious and implacable.

P. JOHN All alone here without a name, how do you know you exist?

SPHINX I wait, therefore I am.

P. JOHN What are you waiting for?

SPHINX You.

P. JOHN Are you going to ask me a riddle?

SPHINX The riddle is the two of us.

P. JOHN I wish I knew your name.

SPHINX I've told you, I haven't got a name. Sphinxes don't have names.

P. JOHN But if you did, it would be a very dignified one. Victoria, perhaps. Or Honoria. Or Penthesilea. Penthesilea Sphinx.

SPHINX You said I smelled of honey.

P. JOHN You do.

SPHINX Honey is sweet, isn't it?

P. JOHN Yes.

SPHINX Well, then.

P. JOHN The long lion-colour of you is like the desert, like an ancient city carved from living rock. Or like a ziggurat.

SPHINX Please . . .

NARRATOR Becoming a ziggurat.

ZIGGURAT . . . not a ziggurat.

P. JOHN What happened?

ZIGGURAT You've zigguratted me. All it took was a word like that to bring out the right angles and the rigid platforms of me. Why were you so poor a John that you had to turn me into architecture?
When the lioness of me, when the honey waited . . .

P. JOHN When the long and lioness of you, the stillness
    and the dance . . .

ZIGGURAT When the Zion of me wanted to remember . . .

P. JOHN . . . the song of you, the lost and golden chance . . .

ZIGGURAT . . . the harp I hung on starlight and the dry
    wind . . .

P. JOHN . . . the sarabands on lost and golden sands . . .

ZIGGURAT . . . the song I sang when we were all
    unknowing . . .

P. JOHN . . . the mystery in your lost and golden hands . . .

BOTH . . . the lost and golden mystery of you and me –

why couldn't I/you be the man you/I wanted me/you to be?
Why did I/you have to be the fool who hesitates and thinks?
Why couldn't I/you be the lover of the sphinx?

P. JOHN You were marvellous as a sphinx. I'll never forget the desert implacability, the hot dry eroticism, the sheer crouchingness of you.

ZIGGURAT It didn't seem to do a lot for you at the time.

P. JOHN There are things one doesn't know until afterwards.

NARRATOR Begins to pace around her.

ZIGGURAT I wish you wouldn't do that. Your circumambulation is loosening the angles and platforms of me. I'm afraid you're going to bring out . . .

NARRATOR She becomes a mirror maze with Poor John on the outside of it.

P. JOHN Where are you?

HERSELF In whatever maze or mystic spiral, labyrinth or
hall of mirrors you may enter,
you will always find me and the mystery of us waiting
for you at the centre;
at any time, in every place, if you come seeking for
my face and ask me where I am,
my answer, night or day, in this or any other way, is
always, 'Here I am.'
Always, everywhere and every who I am, my answer,
even when I don't know what I am, will
still be, 'Here I am.'

P. JOHN All I can see is myself. So many of me!

HERSELF There's no time for reflection; imagine my distress,
trapped in multiplicity and infinite regress –
no longer am I certain of the real time and place of me –
I cannot move until you find the one remembered face of me.

Listen! Do you hear anything?

P. JOHN No.

HERSELF There couldn't be a farmyard around here, could there?

P. JOHN I shouldn't think so.

HERSELF You don't sound any closer.

P. JOHN Although I'm trying very hard to move in your
    direction,
the angle of my incidence is subject to deflection.
This sort of thing could keep me lost for hours or even days,
and at each turning I can feel the terror of the maze.

HERSELF This situation really calls for action somewhat
    stronger –
this centre's going to fall apart, it cannot hold much longer.
Hello, hello, hello! Can you hear me? Now everything's gone
all silent and I don't seem to be anywhere at all.

P. JOHN Are you there? I can't hear you. Hello, hello! O God,
she's gone, without her all the world is desolate and bare,
there's terror in the silence and there's madness in the air,
there's emptiness inside me and there's panic in the bone,
she's left me in this awful maze of mirrors all alone.

NARRATOR Terror approaches him but he doesn't look at her.

TERROR Not alone.

P. JOHN Was that an echo?

TERROR Did it say the same thing you said?

P. JOHN No.

TERROR Then it wasn't an echo.

P. JOHN It must have been one of those sounds I hear
in my head sometimes.

TERROR It was the sound of Terror. Are you afraid?

P. JOHN Of course I'm afraid.

TERROR I go all melty inside when you say that. Say it again.

P. JOHN Of course I'm afraid.

TERROR You sexy thing, you. I like a man who's not afraid
to be afraid. Talk to me, tell me about it.

P. JOHN In certain ways, in certain lights —
it might be days, it might be nights —
there is a time, not night or day . . .

TERROR . . . when meaning seems to drain away,
when all the tower of the mind
lies fallen, and the self can find
no rest, no comfort anywhere,
and in the mirror meets the stare
of its own eyes.

P. JOHN A chilling and a dismal light
that's neither of the day nor night,
a light by which you see your error
reflected in the midnight mirror,
a light in which it's quite a trick
to see yourself and not be sick.

TERROR Go on, say more. I love it when you talk dirty.

P. JOHN When Terror in the midnight mirror,
pale and silent takes its place —
pale and silent shows its face,
see it through a cold white mist
lift its face up to be kissed.

TERROR *Her* face.

P. JOHN Who are you?

TERROR Terror.

P. JOHN Did you say Terror?

TERROR Yes.

P. JOHN Why did you say that?

TERROR That's who I am.

P. JOHN Are you the terror of the mirrors?

TERROR Yes.

P. JOHN The terror of the maze?

TERROR Yes.

P. JOHN The terror of the wrong turning?

TERROR What's a wrong turning?

P. JOHN Well, a turning that gets you lost.

TERROR What about a turning that gets you found?

P. JOHN That's a hard question.

TERROR Turn how you like, there's no way back. Do you feel a cold and brilliant desolation in you?

P. JOHN Yes.

TERROR The mirrors are cold. Cold mirrors under a dismal light. Do you like it that way?

P. JOHN Yes, I like it that way.

TERROR Of course you do;
Terror is a sweet excursion,
other loves are mere perversion.
Terror is the natural vice,
it's stressful but it's very nice;
it keeps you fit, it keeps you active,
keeps you youthful and attractive,
keeps you moving, keeps you pumping
wholesome juices while you're jumping

out of your skin into mine;
feel how smooth it is, how fine!
Love me, bring me what you lack,
love me hard, there's no way back.
Terror, when you're all alone,
is your refuge – to the bone
I will, oh, how I will thrill you,
with my ardour I will chill you
in the most enchanting way,
we can do it night and day –
I will show you new positions,
take you through some strange transitions,
till you reach, with my dark action
soft repose and satisfaction.

P. JOHN I suppose a brief diversion . . .

TERROR Terror is a sweet excursion.

P. JOHN Terror, bring me what I lack,
love me hard, there's no way back.

TERROR Come closer.

NARRATOR Darkness gathers around them.

TERROR Closer yet, closer.

NARRATOR They disappear among the mirrors.

TERROR Shall I . . . ?

P. JOHN Oh, yes, please.

TERROR Yes. That's good, isn't it.

P. JOHN Very good.

TERROR You feel so strong.

P. JOHN My name is Strong John.

TERROR I thought it might be. Tell me how it is for you.

S. JOHN
In this darkness . . .

TERROR

Bright the darkness, dark
the light . . .

in this darkness . . .
there's a dark light in this
darkness . . .

darkly brilliant, darkly
bright . . .

Cold, this dark light . . .

Curving

spacetime curving . . .

curving, twisting like a
snake;
Vanish . . .

Far, far back . . .

a . . .

to that
point of nothing . . .

point of nothing, feel the
sweetness, feel the dread.

Terror, terror, terror, terror,
only terror do I find . . .

Say it, say it, say it, say
it — only Terror in your
mind. Ah, that's it, like that!
So good, my lover! Oh, so
very, very . . . Ahhhh! Was
it good for you?

It was absolutely terrifying.

TERROR I see in you the lineaments of satisfied desire
and shivers run all through me like a river of cold fire.
My darling, I have something to tell you.

S. JOHN What?

TERROR I'm pregnant.

S. JOHN That's nothing to do with me, we've only just met.

TERROR It's everything to do with you, it's your child.

I'm always fertile and I conceive instantaneously. Tomorrow morning I'll give birth and send it round to see its daddy, hoppity-hop.

S. JOHN Hoppity-hop?

TERROR Mmm. Great big hops. Our very own lovechild. Tomorrow morning. If you're true to me.

S. JOHN What do you mean?

TERROR If you were to be unfaithful to me between now and cock-crow the fruit of our union would unconceive itself.

S. JOHN Really!

TERROR But you will be faithful.

S. JOHN Of course.

TERROR You'll be faithful because I'm putting all carnal thoughts out of your mind until after cock-crow. And you'll forget what I've just said and everything else that's happened between us until my spell wears off. Then you'll remember. Daddy.

S. JOHN Then I'll remember. O God.

TERROR But for now it's our secret that nobody knows except me.

NARRATOR Kisses him, goes off. Strong John is listening for something but doesn't look behind him.

S. JOHN What am I listening for? Is there something following me? I think I'd rather not look.

NARRATOR Goes off. We see Herself at the centre of the maze, looking into mirrors.

HERSELF Their secret, is it. Poor John with me and Strong John with her, is he. I'll Strong John him the next time I see him.

NARRATOR The mirrors fly away.

HERSELF Where am I? The maze is gone and the centre with it. Now there's nothing but a vastness of meaningless desolation.

NARRATOR Boredom shuffles in.

BOREDOM Lie down.

HERSELF What for?

BOREDOM I want to lie down on top of you.

HERSELF Why?

BOREDOM I'm very tired and I don't like to sleep rough.

HERSELF Would you go away, please. I'm waiting for some-one.

BOREDOM I am that someone.

HERSELF Not likely.

BOREDOM I am Boredom, the greatest thing there is.

HERSELF Prove it.

BOREDOM Try to think of something greater.

HERSELF That leads to boredom.

BOREDOM You see?

HERSELF Even if there's nothing greater,
leave me now and bore me later.

BOREDOM No one talks to me that way,
the world is mine and I hold sway
with heads of state, with popes and kings,
and millionaires; all kinds of things
move with me in my ups and downs:
businesses and armies, scholars in their gowns,

duchesses in diamonds, ladies of the night,
dance to my slow rhythm, yield to my vast might,
and if I bore you stiff or silly,
and make you yawn or cackle shrilly,
I nonetheless will sing my song,
and if I bore you short or long,
or bore you flat or round or square,
and if I make you tear your hair,
and madly bay the rising moon,
that is my right – I call the tune,
and if you want to know my game,
it's boredom, and my name's the same.
Refrain: With a ho, with a hum, with a tum-te-tum,
with a ho, with a hum, with a tum-te-tum.

HERSELF Refrain: With a him, with a her, with a . . .

NARRATOR She falls asleep. Darkness comes.

BOREDOM She sleeps.

NARRATOR Climbs on top of her.

BOREDOM Everybody needs a little excitement now and then.

NARRATOR Strong John arrives on the scene.

S. JOHN Hello, hello, hello!

BOREDOM Boredom interruptus! Who are you?

S. JOHN Strong John is my name. Take your filthy boring
self off her, you boring thing, you.

NARRATOR They fight.

BOREDOM Ow, ow, ow! Ohhhh!

NARRATOR Boredom is off.

S. JOHN You're safe now, he won't bother you again.

NARRATOR Lights. Herself in Strong John's arms.

116

HERSELF Thank God you've come!

S. JOHN Was it awful for you? Did he . . . ?

HERSELF No, he was very slow. How can I thank you?

S. JOHN I haven't the faintest idea.

HERSELF Is this the next morning or is it still the same day?

S. JOHN It's the same day for me but I don't know what it is for you.

HERSELF You haven't heard anything, have you?

S. JOHN Like what?

HERSELF The cry of a chicken?

S. JOHN The cry of a chicken!

HERSELF A male chicken, actually.

S. JOHN A male chicken is a cock.

HERSELF That's the word I was groping for.

S. JOHN Cocks don't cry, they crow.

HERSELF Right, crowing is what I'm talking about. Have you heard any?

S. JOHN Your question disturbs me strangely. Why are you asking?

HERSELF I seem to need to know. *Have* you heard a cock crowing?

S. JOHN No, but perhaps I wasn't listening. Now I'm going to worry about it.

HERSELF What were you doing while you weren't listening?

S. JOHN I was lost in the mirror maze trying to find you.

HERSELF You don't reek the same as usual.

S. JOHN How do I reek?

HERSELF Of Terror.

S. JOHN I was terribly worried about you.

HERSELF Oh, yes? And how was it?

S. JOHN How was what?

HERSELF You know what. Was it good for you, Strong John?

S. JOHN I can't remember anything at all. Why'd you call me Strong John?

NARRATOR She hits him.

S. JOHN Why'd you do that?

HERSELF Maybe you don't know but I do.

S. JOHN You're a hard hitter, my head's still going round.

HERSELF Maybe it'll come round to a better place than it was in before.

S. JOHN It's coming to a place I can't remember, a forgotten place where we had no story.

HERSELF We had no story, we were just what we were . . .

S. JOHN . . . in the green, in the dim . . .

HERSELF . . . in the place there's no going back to, in the place that's gone.

S. JOHN Then there was an island where I was . . .

MONSTROUS OFFSTAGE VOICE *Caliban*!

HERSELF Who said that?

CALIBAN Nobody. It was one of those sounds you hear in your head. I was Caliban and you were Miranda, there was . . .

BOTH ... the island of our time together,
the past we've never had,
the sea where we swam naked,
the times when we were glad ...

CALIBAN ... when you danced sarabands on golden
     sand ...

MIRANDA ... you were the shadow side of darkness
and the night's left hand.

CALIBAN If we could find our island in that time outside
of time ...

MIRANDA You know there's no going back.

CALIBAN It wouldn't be going back: the time we never
lived is still ahead of us. If we can find our island we can
have that time.

MIRANDA Why are you looking over your shoulder like
that?

MONSTROUS OFFSTAGE VOICE *Caliban*!

MIRANDA It's that awful voice again. Who is it?

CALIBAN It's a thing that's been following me.

M.O.V. LET'S BE HAVING YOU CALIBAN! I'VE BEEN ON YOUR TRACK
FOR A LONG TIME AND I WANT YOU NOW, NOW, NOW!

CALIBAN Who are you?

M.O.V. HERE'S MY CARD.

NARRATOR A big signboard flies in.

MIRANDA Nandical Global Unlimited. That's the company
Ferdinand works for.

CALIBAN (to M.O.V.) What do you want with me?

M.O.V. WE WANT YOU TO BE VICE-PRESIDENT IN CHARGE OF

SALES FOR SELECTED UPWARD-MOBILE WOG TERRITORIES. WE'LL GIVE YOU A HUNDRED THOUSAND A YEAR PLUS A BIG OFFICE AND A GORGEOUS SECRETARY AND A COMPANY CAR AND A GOLD-PLATED KEY TO THE EXECUTIVE TOILET. HOW ABOUT IT?

CALIBAN Daniel Barenboim gets a lot more than that.

M.O.V. CAN YOU PLAY THE PIANO?

CALIBAN No.

M.O.V. WELL, THERE YOU HAVE IT. TAKE LESSONS AND YOUR FUTURE WITH NANDICAL GLOBAL IS UNLIMITED. THINK IT OVER. I'LL GET BACK TO YOU IN FORTY-FIVE SECONDS.

MIRANDA What will you do?

CALIBAN Caliban, Calibonely,
oh so very green and lonely,
green and lonely, deep and mad
Caliban, calibendous
In my huge and my tremendous, in my
slow gigantic changes like the sea, like the sand,
I'm the shadow side of darkness,
I'm the night's left hand.

M.O.V. ACTUALLY WE HAVEN'T SURVEYED THE LEFT-HANDED ETHNIC MARKET. WE'RE ALWAYS OPEN TO NEW POSSIBILITIES.

CALIBAN Can you see my left hand?

NARRATOR Makes a gesture.

M.O.V. IN THAT CASE, BRO, WE'LL HAVE TO TERMINATE YOUR GREEN ASS.

NARRATOR Machine-gun fire. Miranda and Caliban hit the dirt and crawl away.

MIRANDA Which way is the sea?

CALIBAN I don't know but we'll find it.

NARRATOR Artillery barrage begins. Shells explode all around them.

MIRANDA Do you think we'll make it to the island?

CALIBAN The island is wherever we're together.

NARRATOR Big explosion close by.

MIRANDA Did you hear anything just then?

CALIBAN Like what?

MIRANDA Like a male chicken?

CALIBAN I love it when you talk dirty.

NARRATOR Grabs her and pulls her into a shell-hole.

CALIBAN There aren't any chickens around here, there's nobody here but us Calibans and Mirandas.

MIRANDA Strange like the sea you are, strange like the darkness, strange like the sea-shapen rocks of the shore.

BOTH Now we are one thing, we are the wild green, we are the green sea that heaves its great back under bird cry and wing-swoop and wind, we are the great sea that booms in the spout-holes and crashes in echoing caves of the shore. Now we are quiet, now we are deep, deep, deep, deep.

CALIBAN I am the stranger, the dark one, the diver . . .

MIRANDA . . . the shadow side of darkness and the night's left hand.

CALIBAN And in this hand the stars I hold, the sea, the white fog on the water, dark of love, deep mirror of the mystery, you.

MIRANDA I am the mirror where you become small in your mind, great in me.

Show me myself.

CALIBAN Sarabands you dance on golden sands . . .

MIRANDA Sarabands I dance on golden sands,
and mystery, and chance, and in my hands
are golden moments, golden evenings by the sea
and golden moons, and we
two are each other, you and I,
one thing for ever.

CURTAIN

ESSAYS AND SKETCHES

Pan Lives

Eelbrook Common, and evening coming on. Boys with a football in the blue-grey dusk in the empty paddling pond. Black ideographs on the dry grey concrete of the dry and winter paddling pond. A scrawl of boys, a scribble on the dry grey concrete, black against the blue-grey dusk. The dusk purpling a little behind the black trees. The trees on Eelbrook Common are not the same as loose trees, random trees. The trees on Eelbrook Common enclose, enfold, embrace the time, the light, the space, the airs of morning, winds of evening, cries of night on Eelbrook Common. Golden headlamps of the District Line approach with gleams of sliding gold along the curving rails from Parson's Green. The flanged iron wheels rumble on the rails. Steel they may be, but iron is before steel, iron is elemental. There is the idea of iron in the train wheels, the rails of the District Line snaking round the curve speak themselves in iron. There is a rosy blur of westering light behind the darkening silhouettes, behind the blocks of dusk and buildings. Red lights, green lights, a cluster of white and yellowish lamps on the Parson's Green station platform. Stains of yellowish light down corrugated iron, down various wooden slants and angles by the station. Stains of light like rust stains down the sides of iron freighters long at sea. The richness of the deep blue-grey above the westering pink, a blue-grey seen in old picture books, a blue-grey by Edmund Dulac. Wings of night and golden domes in that blue-grey; safe good nights and wooden stairs to bed. The white sparks flashing as the flanged wheels with their carriages recede towards Parson's Green. The blue-grey deepens more and more towards night. The golden windows of the District Line rumble townwards, rumble homewards through the deepening dark. The buildings mass themselves against the night, stand up in solid black behind the black trees on the common. Behind those blacks the dusk commits itself with deepening blue to night as all at once the white lights of the football pitch come on. Overhead an aeroplane slants droning evenwards to Heathrow. And still the layers of the last blue daylight can be seen between the blocks of dark like mortar in the bricks of night. To those passing on foot or in the carriages of the District Line this window where I sit is one of evening's golden windows. Here behind that golden window six-and-a-half-year-old Jake dances to the music of Ravi Shankar. From the gramophone the sitar, the tabla, the tanpura thump and drone and buzz and jangle. Jake laughs as he dances like a little Shiva. The music makes him dance, he says; he can't help it.

I've just described the coming of evening to Eelbrook Common as seen from my window. I used language to do it. It seems to me, however, that what I was describing was itself language, all of it, from the blackness of the trees to my son's dancing. I was using our little language of words to describe the big language of nightfall. To me it seems that everything that happens is language, everything that goes on is saying something.

Well, you might say, what difference does it make, really, if someone chooses to call everything language? It's only a manner of speaking. It's only words. Only words, you might say. Because although we recognise words as our only official language we don't attach too much importance to them. Words are only words. In my description of nightfall on Eelbrook

Common the events are familiar ones: our part of the earth is turning away from the sun; the trains of the District Line are taking people home; boys are playing football in the empty paddling pond and so on. It's pretty much what happens every evening between five-thirty and six. We all know pretty well where we are with it and we don't really need to bother about what to call it. The words don't matter all that much.

And yet, you see, there's more to it. Keep in mind what St John says: 'In the Beginning was the Word, and the Word was with God, and the Word was God.' I think that idea is in us independently of Christianity; I think it's simply in us and inexplicable. Keep in mind St John and keep in mind the scrawl, the scribble, the graffito of boys in the dry and winter paddling pond. At the same time move with me to another picture in my mind: a school yard full of small boys on a cold grey January afternoon. Jake had forgotten his swimming trunks and I had brought them for him. I came through a narrow passage into a brick-walled space of concrete sudden with boys like migrant warblers blown against a lighthouse. O, the sadness of childhood! Not that the boys were being sad. They were running, scuffling, fighting, or standing about as if they had been caught in a wild state and herded into that enclosure. Jake was being some kind of large slow bird, a stork or a crane perhaps. He was flapping slowly and peacefully singing to himself as he circled the yard. But ah, the sadness of childhood in all those little boys!

Returning to the Gospel of St John: 1.1. 'The Word was with God, and the Word was God.' 1.14. 'And the Word was made flesh.' The Word here is the Greek *Logos*. *Logos* means both word and reason, and in the Gospel of St John the *Logos* is nothing less than God. Can God and word and reason be thought of separately? Obviously not. (When I talk of God here I don't mean any particularised denominational God, I mean the primal force and mover of the cosmos, I mean the universal mind, I mean whatever it is that pervades the universe and requires us to take notice of it.) If God is the origin of all things then word and reason along with everything else must come from God. That being so, any thinking about language will necessarily be religious thinking. Any thinking about *anything* will necessarily be religious thinking, but it's language that we're concentrating on now, language and the sadness of childhood and the Word made flesh.

What is this language that I'm insisting on? The sky grows dark, the trains rumble towards Wimbledon, towards Upminster, boys play football in an empty paddling pond and I call that language. Why? Because there is a continual telling and asking going on, a continuous conversation that is trying to happen between everything around us and us. All of it is without words, much of it is silent. Listen, look, let it come to you – the turning of the earth away from Father Sun to Mother Night, the rolling of our cloud-wreathed planet in the vasty deeps of space. Enormities of space and gathered night all round and yet the trees are saying the blackness of themselves, the purple of the sky all round them. You can hear it in your throat if you look attentively. That rumbling of the trains, that mumbling of the iron wheels on the iron rails – if you were to invent a rolling-through-darkness sound it would be that sound, wouldn't it, the sound of tunnelling human-kind rolling home through the dark, rolling on iron wheels under the earth, willing to endure a double darkness, willing to exchange the light of the dusk for the speed of the tunnel. Through the rock and through the dark with lighted windows swaying, faces entranced, speaking mysteries of silence. For God's sake, for the sake of the Word that is God, hear it say itself, hear the murmurous silence of the daily Word made flesh. Hear the earth say itself, say itself ponderous with evening, turning to the night while little Words of flesh kick a football in the empty paddling pond. All of it needs to be taken in not as event but as language, as the allness of everything saying itself to us because we are what it talks to.

What has the sadness of childhood to do with language? Can we agree that there *is* a sadness in childhood? Can we agree that sometimes in a quiet moment when you look at a child in the grey light from a window you will feel a pang in your heart? Is it the thought of how small the child is and how big everything else is that lies beyond the window? Yes, I think that's in it. But I think it's mostly something else that gives the sadness, something on this side of the window, something with all of us right now: time. Time that will one day take away even this little child who is now so very young and new and not at all tired. This child must, like all children, grow old and die and that gives us the heart pang, that makes us sad. That's the heart of the matter, isn't it? Out of the silence for a little time and back into it again for ever.

The child by the window is not thinking of the brevity of life, the child has as yet no idea of it. Time! The child has all the time in the world, time to look at everything without hurrying, time to be intimately concerned with string and the space behind the sofa and the traffic of ants and beetles. There is a sadness in that too, in the child's not knowing how little time there is. Or is the sadness in our not knowing how *much* there is? Do we miss our grip on the moments of our life, do we lose time that we could find? Is our language of words reductive?

For example: my five-year-old son Ben comes to my desk, climbs on to my lap, and shows me a fountain brush he's borrowed from me. It's a Japanese-style brush with a hollow handle in which there's a reservoir of ink. 'Look,' says Ben. He finds a bit of paper with a clear space on it, draws something abstract with the brush and colours it in. 'Look,' says Ben. 'With a pen you get a little little thin line but with this one it just goes *blup!* So fast it comes out and you can colour in a whole lot all at once. Why is that?' I say, 'It's because of the way the ink flows off the brush. Brushes are made so that ink or paint will flow off them like that.'

'Yes,' says Ben. 'That's what it is: it flows.' He is strongly satisfied at putting the word *flow* to the action he has just described. The one word takes in all of the phenomena involved when ink comes off a brush on to a sheet of paper. It comes to my mind while saying that that I have read in one of Lafcadio Hearn's translations from the Japanese of a god of ink, or at least a spirit of ink – some personification, at any rate, of ink, some being responsive to prayer, flattery, or propitiation; something in the ink that makes it come on to the paper dull or clever, beautiful or ugly. Certainly those of us who use ink and paper daily would pray to such a god if we knew its name.

This is what always happens as soon as you pause even for a moment to look at anything at all: you suddenly have many, many things to ponder. And while I write this, the evening, another evening, again says itself, speaks itself, tells itself on Eelbrook Common. Along the District Line the red lights and the green, the yellow and the white arrange themselves as the trees go dark. The violet evening seems to sit in perfect stillness, as if entranced with itself, before the mirror of the sky.

I worry a little – and yet why should I worry? – about Ben's now having the word *flow* in his mind instead of what was there before. The ignorance that was there before was in its way a *religious* ignorance – the person was in a respectful relationship to something not fully understood, the person was respectfully offering the mind to the thing, was holding the mind open to all of the thing. Now he doesn't know any more than he did before but he has a word to call it by. Will he think less about what the word refers to now? I look at my child in the grey light from the window and I think: Can there come a time when he will perceive only those things there are words for? No, not Ben. Not my Ben. And yet everybody was somebody's somebody as a child, and as a child must have lived in religious ignorance like Ben.

The people who run the world now were children once. What went wrong? What is it that with such dismal regularity goes wrong? Why do perfectly good children become rotten grown-ups? If I say there's a language failure somewhere does that make any sense? Keep in mind my claim that everything is language. Am I saying then that there's an everything failure? Yes, because nothing has a chance of working right when people won't listen to what it says and with the proper action say the right things back. Go from the big to the little for a moment. Go in your mind from the world to your own body. Can there by now be anyone who doubts that the body is continually talking to us? You say to your head, 'We're going to that party tonight and we're going to smile and talk to all those people we don't want to smile and talk to.' Your head says, 'Ache ache ache.' You say to your gall bladder, 'I'm so bitter, life is so hard!' Your gall bladder says, 'If you feel that way about it I'll commemorate it with a stone.' Your heart says, 'I am heavy. I have no ease. You are doing things with only half of me. You are not doing what is close to me. You are following a path without me. I am not in good self. I have no self for what you're doing. You have not gone to the me of the matter. I feel attacked. Maybe I'll attack you.' When your heart says that of course you'll listen, because by then you're probably getting pains down your left arm and let's hope your local emergency ward isn't on strike. Language! Twenty-four hours a day, fourteen hundred and forty minutes daily, eighty-six thousand, four hundred seconds from dawn to dawn our bodies are talking to us. Now go from the little to the big, from the body we live in to the world we live in: trees and buildings, mountains and cinemas and supermarkets and oceans – all of it, complete with sky and weather. All of it, I insist, is talking to us. How could it be otherwise? Ugliness shrieks and gabbles; beauty sings, growls, whispers; the everyness of days bellows like a dying bull;

the dead leaves rattle, the madness of nations crouches in its newsprint and chatters its teeth. The stones cry out to be spoken to and we must find a language base from which to respond.

Language base, I said. The idea of a language base has been in my mind for nearly half a year now and I know it's important. I don't understand it fully but I know it's not just an idea – it's something real and it's something that matters. I'll tell you how this idea came to me. It happened in September 1978 on the Greek island of Paxos, which was of course the proper place for it to happen, and I'll tell you why.

Robert B. Palmer, in his introduction to his translation of Walter F. Otto's book *Dionysus, Myth and Cult*, discusses the history in literature of Pan. He quotes Elizabeth Barrett Browning and Plutarch. The Elizabeth Barrett Browning lines are from 'The Dead Pan' – lines which she herself says were partly 'Excited by Schiller's *Götter Griechenlands*, and partly founded on a well-known tradition mentioned in a treatise of Plutarch according to which, at the hour of the Saviour's agony, a cry of "Great Pan is dead!" swept across the waves in the hearing of certain mariners – and the oracles ceased.' Mrs Browning went on to write a poem that gloats over the passing of Pan and the old gods. She says, in Stanza XXXIV:

> Earth outgrows the mythic fancies
> Sung beside her in her youth:
> And those debonaire romances
> Sound but dull beside the truth.
> Phoebus' chariot-course is run.
> Look up, poets, to the sun!
> Pan, Pan is dead.

Palmer's introduction starts with the opening stanza of Mrs Browning's poem:

Gods of Hellas, gods of Hellas,
Can ye listen in your silence?
Can your mystic voices tell us
Where ye hide? In floating islands,
With a wind that evermore
Keeps you out of sight of shore?
      Pan, Pan is dead.

Palmer continues: 'When Elizabeth Barrett Browning wrote these lines which sound so pessimistic and so limited to any lover of the beauty and truth of Greek mythology, she had in mind a famous passage out of Plutarch's *De Oraculorum Defectu* in which it was reported on good authority that Pan had died.'

Palmer then lets Philip tell the story:

As for death among such beings [the deities], I have heard the words of a man who was not a fool nor an impostor. The father of Aemilianus the orator, to whom some of you have listened, was Epitherses, who lived in our town and was my teacher in grammar. He said that once upon a time, in making a voyage to Italy, he embarked on a ship carrying freight and many passengers. It was already evening when, near the Echinades Islands, the wind dropped, and the ship drifted near Paxi. Almost everybody was awake, and a good many had not finished their after-dinner wine. Suddenly from the island of Paxi was heard the voice of someone loudly calling Thamus, so that all were amazed. Thamus was an Egyptian pilot, not known by name even to many on board. Twice he was called and made no reply, but the third time he answered; and the caller, raising his voice, said, 'When you come opposite to Palodes, announce that Great Pan is dead.' On hearing this, all, said Epitherses, were astonished and reasoned among themselves whether it was better to carry out the order or to refuse to meddle and let the matter go. Under the circumstances Thamus made up his mind that if there should be a breeze, he would sail past and keep quiet, but with no wind and a smooth sea about the place, he would announce what he had heard. So, when he came opposite Palodes, and there was neither wind nor wave, Thamus, from the stern, looking toward the land, said the words as he had heard them: 'Great Pan is dead.' Even before he had finished, there was a great cry of lamentation, not of one person, but of many, mingled with exclamations of amazement.

This event occurred supposedly in the first century AD, during the reign of Tiberius, in a Roman world in which the rationalistic and evolutionistic approach to religion had already done much to bring death not only to Pan but to many of the other greater and lesser gods of the Greek pantheon. Later, however, Christian legend was to suggest that Pan had died on the very day when Christ had mounted the cross. It is this later tradition which leads to the hymn of triumph with which Mrs Browning's poem ends. Now Mrs Browning's last stanza:

> Oh brave poets, keep back nothing,
> Nor mix falsehood with the whole!
> Look up Godward, speak the truth in
> Worthy song from earnest soul;
> Hold, in high poetic duty,
> Truest Truth the fairest Beauty!
> Pan, Pan is dead.'

There I shall leave Palmer's introduction so that I can move on to the subject of the language base. I must pause, however, to offer the last stanza of Schiller's lament for the passing of the old gods, the poem to which Mrs Browning's poem was a reply:

> Yes, they did go home, and everything beautiful,
> Everything high they took away with them,
> All colours, all sounds of life,

And for us remained only the de-souled Word.
Torn out of the time-flood, they float
Saved on the heights of Pindus;
What undying in song shall live
Must in life go under.

On the island of Paxos they just throw the garbage down
the hillsides. I don't know what they did before Pan died but
that's what they do now. Over the terrace, *blup!* Beautiful
Ionian island in the sparkling blue sea and it's got plastic
mineral-water bottles all over it. There was a yellow plastic
meat-grinder blooming by the roadside – we used to pass it
every day – it was slowly working its way into the town.
Thrown-away cookers rusting in the olive groves. Black
donkeys braying, heehawing in mysterious green-lit olive
groves. Goats. Goats and donkeys, they're not big, they
don't have to be big, they are the familiars of the really
big things. Look at a goat's eyes, listen to a donkey bray.
Magic. Cocks crowing among the rusting iron in the olive
groves. Magic. Stones. Stones walling the terraces, stones
islanding the olive trees, dry stones holding the earth to the
hillsides. Stones. Broken stones and bits of stone. Some are
sand-coloured, some are grey, some are white. Some look like
curtains of stone, some look like broken monuments. Very
good for writing on or drawing on – the ink goes on to the
stone as if it were prehistoric. Mostly I drew on the road
stones and wrote on the beach stones. The beach stones are all
kinds of rounded shapes and some of them fit together in
strange ways. The olive trees, of course, they produce olives.
You can see the olives like black dots in a vase painting, black
against the blue sky. But it isn't just olives growing on the
trees, there's the light. Light lives in those olive trees: it
flashes and glimmers like a shoal of fish turning where the
sun slants through the green sea. Light sings and twitters
in the silvery-green leaves like birds. O yes, there's more
to olive trees than olives. The blue sky through the green,

135

through the silver leaves, the green light in the groves, the whispering, the twittering of the sunlight in the leaves. Whispering, conversing, beckoning. Very, very old, some of those olive trees. Old and hollow, gnarled and twisted, holding themselves open like magical garments, showing the ancient hollow darkness in them. They look as if they might have nymphs, dryads, gods or demons inside them. Twisting their roots into the ground, holding open their hollow darkness for someone, something, to go in, come out. Olive trees producing light effects, breeze effects. Black donkeys get tied to the olive trees. Perhaps the donkeys are the familiars of the spirit indwelling in the olive tree. Perhaps each olive grove has its genius who has a black donkey for its familiar and the black donkey has an oracle-eyed goat for his communicant who in turn listens to the crowing of a cock in the middle of the night, before dawn, at dawn, at midday, at dreamy noon when Pan sleeps. Because Pan isn't dead, don't think that for a moment. There are no dead gods. Bel, Marduk, Tiamat, they're all with us still: every god that was ever named and worshipped, not one of them is dead. No god is ever supplanted, no god ever becomes obsolete. Pan lives, he makes his music on the hills and in the groves he stamps his cloven hooves and dances.

The house we stayed in on Paxos looked as if it had been stained long ago with the juice of red and purple berries. It had a red-tiled roof. It had a flagged courtyard. There was a table under a grape arbour. There were orange trees and a pomegranate tree.

Water for the house came from a cistern that was the same colour as the house: it was a little square building with steps going up to the low flat roof of it. There was a long pipe from the roof gutters of the house to the cistern. When it rained the water ran through the pipe into the cistern. There was a pump on the cistern. Whenever a tap was turned on or the toilet was flushed the pump would gasp and pant as it pumped water into the pipes of the house. It whined and howled and panted like an animal by day, a beast of work. At night it was like a dark brother howling in the courtyard while mopeds traced a line of putter up the hill past a little chapel.

It came to me while listening to that pump one night that it was foolish to make too many distinctions between the animate and the inanimate; everything was talking, the world was full of constant language. What did all the language mean? It meant itself, that's all, and itself was something I knew. I didn't know it the way you know something to tell about it but the knowing was in me. There is no sound, no silence, no pattern of sound and silence that will not correspond to something in your head. Try it some time: find the farthest-out record of the most avant-garde electronic music or whatever is the most alien and chaotic sound for you. Listen to it a few times; very quickly the blips and bleeps become orderly and familiar, become the voice and language of something that was in you waiting for that music. However random the composer tries to be, it's impossible to compose sound that has no pattern: anything you hear is a pattern of sound-waves and every pattern refers to all other patterns; everything is some kind of information. The universe is continually communicating itself to us in a cosmic eucharist of waves and particles.

So there I was in what you might call a state of aroused language response. I sensed that I was in a better place with language than I'd been before. I was writing a letter to a daughter thousands of miles away. I could feel that even before a word was said I was further out into the world than words had ever taken me before. The communion with the donkeys, the stones, the goats, the olive trees had given me a language base more advanced than I had had before.

How to explain it? What is the language fabric of olive trees and cisterns, pumps and donkeys, stones in the road, plastic mineral-water bottles, sunlight in the leaves, water rushing through the pipes? It is that continual transmutation I have described; it is everything for ever in the process of becoming everything. In that process the language base is both a place and a relationship; it is where you are to everything that isn't you – stones and olive trees and donkeys, everything: Pan. Pan, a god not much revered, not always taken seriously in books, a lewd and rustic god. His name means *all, everything*. From his name comes the word *panic*, the panic of the all-terror, the everything-terror. Half-human, half-animal is Pan – horned man, goat below the waist, potent with animality, standing his ground with animal hooves. A shepherd's god, he is the Old Word of the groves and hills, and the legend has him dead when the New Word, Christ, rises on the cross. One source equates him with demons, another with the Christ who supplants him and all the high gods of Olympus. With the reed that was the body of the nymph Syrinx, the object of his unsatisfied lust, he makes music. A humble god, an intimate, a *Thou* who whispers in the wind in the leaves, howls with the pump on the cistern. Why cannot he die? Why cannot any god die? Because gods do not replace one another. Let prophets and kings do what they will: gods are a cumulative projection of everything in us. I'm not trying to reduce this to psychiatry – I mean that we worship the gods projected by the god-force that projects us as well on the screen of its mind. Gods and no-gods are a cumulative projection, and, as we well know, the most monstrous of the gods are alive and present in us equally with the most gentle of them: the new and the old jostle for place in a continually shifting balance. If there is conservation of energy and conservation of matter how could there not be conservation of God?

Pan, the *all*, the *everything* half-human, half-animal god, is there to be a *Thou* for us to talk to. Because that's what the language base is. It's a place where the *Thou* of things is perceived and the silence speaks. The best that words can do is to make a space in which the silence can speak, in which the language of the everything can be heard. Humankind is naturally and properly religious, and I suggest that one definition of religion is that it is a mode of being and perception in which everything is *Thou* and nothing is *It*. Certainly we've tried the other way; we've tried making both things and people *It*, and we've seen the results.

Is it possible that the sadness we sense in childhood is the sadness of the *Thou* perceivers who know that the world will come between them and the *Thou* of things, will stop its mouth and their ears? Is it the sadness of the listener who will not be allowed to hear the silence speak? Or is the sadness something else? Is it that whatever looks out through the child's eyes knows that it must destroy the child to make the adult, must close the garden of the child to the grown-up just as Adam and Eve closed Eden to themselves? Is the sadness of the child the knowledge that it is doomed to repeat the original sin, deny its knowledge of the *Thou*, kill humble Pan and crucify the Word?

I look at the back of Ben's neck as he kneels on the floor cutting out something with quite a large pair of scissors. He's very good with scissors; he can cut string with a razor blade without cutting himself; he uses a hammer and a bolster well. He's very patient about all the heavy tools and delicate equipment he's not yet allowed to use. And yet I can't know what might be in him waiting to rise up towering like a giant mushroom-shaped cloud. The Japanese called the bomb that fell on Hiroshima *Gensu Makkadan*, 'the Original Child Bomb'. Well, it's a chance you take when you decide to have children and keep the human race going. There was a toy sold a few years back, a box with an on-off switch. When you switched it on a little hand came out of the box and switched it off.

A cold noonday on Eelbrook Common. A train recedes to Parson's Green, the tracks are empty. The sky is bleak, a cold wind flattens last year's dead leaves against the wire netting of the football pitch. The dry paddling pond is empty of boys. The wind stirs the bare March branches. But I know that under Eelbrook Common runs a secret Eelbrook with its olive groves. Soon I shall hear the tawny owl at night, and in his London voice will be another voice, that far Ionian pump, dark brother to the cistern.

1983

Household Tales by
The Brothers Grimm

Introduction to 1977 Picador Edition

When I was a child it never occurred to me to wonder where these tales came from; they were simply there on the shelf waiting for me. Their first name was *Grimm's*, their middle name was *Fairy*, their last name was *Tales*, and that was that. Only in recent years have I come to know – I think it was my wife who told me – that Jacob Grimm (1785–1863) and Wilhelm Grimm (1786–1859) did not make up any of the stories; they went around collecting them from people who knew them by heart, had learnt them as a common resource passed from one generation to the next.

It's strange how a body of experience newly connected with a fact becomes new experience. Some of these tales I haven't read for years and years; many of them are altogether new to me. Now when I read them I feel the strands of story come into my mind as I might feel with my hands the weights and textures of ropes of pearls and ropes of sand, ropes of onions, thick hairy ropes of hemp, and fine silk threads and ribbons. Pearls and onions don't come out of nowhere.

I wasn't particularly looking for origins when I sat down to read these forty-seven tales so that I could write this introduction. I was simply pottering along quietly, making notes and waiting for something to happen. When something did happen it turned out to be the somewhere of a story's origin, revealing itself with startling swiftness and clarity and starting new thoughts in me.

It happened while I was reading 'The Goose-Girl'. If you haven't read that story lately you should read it now before going on with this. I'll wait here.

My first notes after reading the story are:
Why had she no escort other than the maid-in-waiting? So that she'd be vulnerable? So the story could happen? Story is affecting out of proportion to events in it. Fall from high state to low one. False taken for true. Severed head. Speaking head. A gateway. A passage. An entrance and exit. A place for going in and out . . .

The head of the horse Falada in 'the great dark-looking gateway' has made me feel the dark shapes moving in the darks of time, darks of earth. The idea of severed heads that talk is in us; when we meet it in a story there is no shock of surprise.

With dictionary in hand I go to the original German text. There the maid-in-waiting, the false bride, tells her husband to call the *Schinder*, the knacker, who will '*den Hals abhauen*', the neck cut off. In the English translation it's 'cut off the head'.

Curious about the use of *neck* instead of *head* in the original, I get the one-volume abridgement of *The Golden Bough** off the shelf to see what Frazer has to say about animal sacrifice. On p.618, after citing the ritual sacrifice of goats, oxen, and pigs, Frazer says:

> . . . to put it generally, the corn-spirit is killed in animal form in autumn; part of his flesh is eaten as a sacrament by his worshippers; and part of it is kept till next sowing time or harvest as a pledge and security for the continuance

*Macmillan Paperback 1957. (*The Golden Bough* was first published in twelve volumes in 1890; the abridgement was first published in 1922.)

or renewal of the corn-spirit's energies.

... in the cave of Phigalia in Arcadia the Black Demeter was portrayed with the head and mane of a horse on the body of a woman ... The legend told of the Phigalian Demeter indicates that the horse was one of the animal forms assumed in ancient Greece, as in modern Europe, by the corn-spirit. It was said that in her search for her daughter (Persephone) Demeter assumed the form of a mare to escape the addresses of Poseidon, and that, offended at his importunity, she withdrew in dudgeon to a cave not far from Phigalia in the highlands of Western Arcadia. There, robed in black, she tarried so long that the fruits of the earth were perishing, and mankind would have died of famine if Pan had not soothed the angry goddess and persuaded her to quit the cave. In memory of this event, the Phigalians set up an image of the Black Demeter in the cave; it represented a woman dressed in a long robe, with the head and mane of a horse. The Black Demeter, in whose absence the fruits of the earth perish, is plainly a mythical expression of the bare wintry earth stripped of its summer mantle of green.

Working back to p.603 I find:

Sometimes the corn-spirit appears in the shape of a horse or mare. Between Kalw and Stuttgart, when the corn bends before the wind, they say, 'There runs the Horse'. At Bohlingen, near Radolfzell in Baden, the last sheaf of oats is called the Oats-Stallion. In Hertfordshire, at the end of the reaping, there is, or used to be, observed a ceremony called 'crying the Mare'. The last blades of corn left standing on the field are tied together and called the Mare. The reapers stand at a distance and throw their sickles at it; he who cuts it through 'has the prize, with acclamations and good cheer'.

Elsewhere Frazer tells us that in Devon and Cornwall the

last sheaf of the harvest is called 'the neck'; '*nack*' in Devon dialect. That takes me back to the word *knacker*. *The Oxford English Dictionary* defines knacker as horse-slaughterer, and says that the origin of the word is obscure. It seems to me not at all unlikely that the word originally referred to the one who cut the horse's neck. In any case it was the German word for neck that put me on the track of Demeter and Persephone. Words have a way of doing that. Symbols change with time and place; the last sheaf of the harvest gathered many names, some of them echoed in 'The Goose-Girl': sometimes the last sheaf was 'the gander's neck', sometimes it was 'the bride'. In some places a corn-puppet was ritually stripped as the princess in the tale was stripped of her finery by the maid-in-waiting; in other places the woman who bound the last sheaf was called 'the Wheat-bride'.

Back beyond the symbols stand other symbols; the names and sexes vary in a palimpsest of myth and history: back beyond Demeter and Persephone stand Isis and Osiris in Egyptian myth, Tammuz and Inanna in Sumerian. Beyond Dionysus torn in pieces at Thebes, beyond the body of Osiris dismembered we find the grim recall of human beings ritually slaughtered on the harvest-field. What is in us must be looked at.

Now consider the main elements of 'The Goose-Girl'. Like Demeter and Persephone there are an old queen and her daughter, a '*Jungfer Königin*', virgin queen. The princess is the true bride, the harvest bride promised to the prince. Between the old queen and the young queen there is a blood bond of communication, the little sacrifice of three drops of blood from the old queen's finger which is a little symbolic neck. The harvest bride goes '*weit über Feld*', far over field. With her goes a maid-in-waiting, a season in waiting who strips the harvest bride and replaces her as the winter replaces the season of growth and harvest. The 'false bride', the winter, has the neck of the horse/corn-spirit cut. Through the reign of winter, through the dark time of her reduction to a lower state, her comedown or descent, the true bride, who is both Demeter and Persephone, both harvest bride and young corn-spirit, talks to her Black Demeter corn-spirit mother, the head of Falada. Conrad the goose-boy plainly has designs on her. When the goose-girl, the ripening young virgin queen, undoes her golden hair, '*machte ihre Haare auf*', opened her hair, Conrad would like to pluck a few of those hairs. He'd like to do some premature harvesting. But the promised bride-in-waiting calls on the wind to help her preserve her virginity. When her proper season comes, the true bride creeps into a stove, a womb-like place in which she reveals, like the Pythia at Delphi, the true state of things. The false bride, winter, is driven out and put to death, and the true bride, the young corn-spirit, reigns.

Characteristic of the myth-based tale is the absence of emotion where one would expect to find it. If we look at 'The Goose-Girl' as story alone, we are left wondering about the maid-in-waiting, the 'false bride' who married the prince. Presumably they've slept together, lived together, had some kind of relationship. But the prince lets her be killed horribly, and apparently without a second thought, when the goose-girl is revealed as his true bride. Because this is not story-story: it is the transmission of mythic elements in story form; it is proto-story.

I don't speak German. My wife, however, is German and has done for me a literal translation of 'The Goose-Girl'. Compare the very first words of the story:

> *Es lebte einmal eine alte Königin . . .*

In this book you'll find that rendered:
Once upon a time there was a Queen . . .

Literally translated it is:
It lived once an old Queen . . .

'It lived once an old Queen . . . ' Even that simple idiom is alive with the earthy awareness that something lives us. We are not an unconnected happening. The original language of these stories is better than any literary translation can hope to be – plain and powerful, quick with life and densely interwoven like an ancient hedge from which peep out the eyes of birds and mice. That steady ongoing voice that passes from one teller to the next resounds with earth and mortal echoes:

> '*O du Falada, da du hangest . . .* '
> '*O du Jungfer Königin, da du gangest . . .* '

Do you hear the earth-feet, loam-feet, dancing slowly and the winds of season after season in that '*da du hangest*'/'*da du gangest*'? Here are blood and earth becoming word-music; here is the quickening of myth into art that lives its own life.

Granted that this folk-tale is descended from a myth, why have I bothered to look for the myth in the folk-tale, and why should you care whether it's there or not?

Consider fiction phenomenologically. The word itself is derived from the past participle of the Latin *fingere*, to shape, fashion, form or mould. We take it for granted that there will always be fiction of one kind or another in the form of stories: forming; shaping. Why do we take that for granted? Why do we make fiction? Why do we say, 'What if?'

We make fiction because we *are* fiction. Because there was a time when 'it lived' us into being. Because there was a time when something said, 'What if there are people?' A word, perhaps, whispered in the undulant amorphous ear of the primordial soup: 'What if there are people, hey? What if?'

It lived us into being and it lives us still. We make stories because we are story. The fabric of our myths and folk-tales is in us from before birth. The action systems of the universe are the origin of life and stories. The patterns of blue-green algae and the numinous wings of the Great Nebula in Orion and the runic scrawl of human chromosomes are stories. Begotten by no one knows what, stories beget people to live them. We are the offspring of immeasurable ideas.

The myths that are in us, whether they be of Demeter/
Persephone's winter descent or Orpheus losing Eurydice,
are the dynamics of thing-in-itself acting itself out in the
collective being and consciousness of which each of us is
a particle. When the goose-girl says:

> 'Falada, Falada, hanging high . . . '

and the head answers:

> 'Princess, Princess, passing by,
> Alas, alas! if thy mother knew it,
> Sadly, sadly, her heart would rue it.'

we thrill to a mysterious sadness that is *familiar*. Even when
we read the story for the first time, it seems not new to us but
a recall of experience that is in us. An evocation rather than a
recall, because the experience is not from a specific past but
is always present in us *now*. As if we always have been and
always are the true bride and the false one and the horse as
well. As if all life and all experience are in all of us. It's as it is
when we dream: the dreamer is all of the people in the dream;
everybody and everything in the dream has been set in motion
by the mind of . . . whom? Whose is the conscious and the
dreaming mind? The physicist Erwin Schrödinger has said:*

> Mind is by its very nature a *singulare tantum*. I should say:
> the overall number of minds is just one. I venture to call
> it indestructible since it has a peculiar timetable, namely
> mind is always *now*. There is really no before and after
> for mind. There is only a now that includes memories and
> expectations. But I grant that our language is not adequate
> to express this, and I also grant, should anyone wish to
> state it, that I am now talking religion, not science . . .

It feels to me as if that's how it is: just one mind, and all

---

***What is Life? AND Mind and Matter*, Cambridge University Press,
1967.

of us know everything. Not intellectually but experientially. All of us have been, all of us are, everything. So if we ask the question: What is it to be us? and look for answers in our myths, we see being as a series of alternations. We have been, and we are, the true bride and the false one. 'Falsely' rejected, we endure our season of darkness; 'falsely' accepted, we enjoy the prince's bed and board; 'rightfully' deposed, we die rolling naked in the nail-studded barrel; 'rightfully' restored to our proper station, we thrive. We live our seasons as our seasons live us because that is the way of the universe: endless cycles of gain and loss, continual exchanges of energy.

No system is static; it is always in the process of becoming what it is not. Any putting-together charges whatever is put together with the energy that will tear it apart. The winding-down of one system is the winding-up of another. The condition is circular: it doesn't matter where you apparently enter the cycle. Be Eurydice lost, and the energy of that system will put together the Orpheus who has lost you and the music with which he will gain entrance to the nether world. Be Orpheus, and the energy of that system will be scattered when the Thracian women tear you apart. Be the Thracian women, and your tearing-apart of Orpheus will release the energy that puts him together again with Eurydice unlost. Eurydice and Orpheus and the Thracian women are only the costumes: the actors are the being lost, the losing and the finding, the gathering and the scattering. The actors are the action cycles continually moving in us and in all things.

If we are being lived by action cycles at the same time in us and beyond us, what is there for us to do? Everything. The action is abstractly *plus* or *minus, yang* or *yin, in* or *out, towards* or *away from.* It is we who clothe the action with ourselves. It is we who decide the character of the action, whether it be, in human terms, vital or deadly.

Around us all is night, black night that howls outside the circle of our words or crouches magically with the fire reflected in its eyes. We are in it; it is in us. We need to know that night and we need not to know. Our primal 'What if?' is the twining of our fingers in the dark with those of unseen Chance and whispering Dread who walk with us. They are sister and brother to us, father and mother: the ancient family of not-knowing, walking in uncertainty.

In that uncertainty our stories go with us on roads of luck and death, of love and lostness. Burn all the books, and still there will be stories. Make a law requiring forty hours of television-watching weekly, and still there will be stories. Charred by fire or burnt out by electronics, stories will put themselves together out of ashes and broken glass and melted wire; and not perhaps such stories as we might like. But they will live us according to their need because we are a fiction, a continual forming and shaping.

That's why it matters that the myths be found and recognised in old and smooth-rubbed stories: to make a fire in the night and a clear space in the silence where the voice of all our past and immanent *now* can sound; to keep us from losing the story of us. We are not a random happening: the seasons of the earth are in us, and the seasons of the galaxies, the tides of the expanding universe as well. We are the true bride and the false one acting out a cycle not of our invention. Perhaps there still is time for us to find a way of doing it with hands shaped to the things of life, with death a natural exchange of rounded strophes rather than a monster madness gabbling in the dark.

That's why Grimm is worth a closer look. These are household tales for a world that is one single household. In these stories we can find our way not back, but forward to the story of us.

You will remember that it was the idea of the horse's head in the gateway that made me wonder about the origins of 'The Goose-Girl'. It isn't at all surprising that horses figure in so many different ways in myth and story – there is such power in them beyond the physical. The prehistoric life in them seems whole and intact. Any horse you meet seems to have in it a knowing that is deeper, older, more primal than our own; they seem witnesses to something lost to the sight of humankind. There is something important about horses. See a great dark carthorse in the rain, steam coming up from its back; go out to a stable in the cold dark of a winter morning: when horses look at you, where they look from is not where we look from. I believe that most of us would like to be thought well of by horses.

Before the motorcar replaced the horse, and for some years after, there were many illustrators who drew horses with the same authority with which they drew the human figure; now there are very few who can do that. Most modern illustrators fudge a horse the best they can and hope to get by on technique. Mervyn Peake's horses are of a piece with his people: some are knaves, some are drudges, and some of them are magical.

The drawing of the goose-girl talking to the head of Falada is a picture that one can look at for a long time. The horse is one of Peake's magical beasts. The great dead eyes are certainly not horse's eyes, they are *other*. They make one think of a deer but also of a praying mantis. They are disquieting, disturbing, disorienting: if a horse has eyes like that, then anything might be almost anything, and gone are the guarantees implicit in the ordinary look of things.

The head of Falada is not realistically nailed to the wall; the neck and head simply grow out of the wall that divides a world of shadow from a world of light. The dense hatching of the shadow side of the wall seems the particulate face of time itself. Through the archway stream the white geese into the light on the distant meadows and hills.

The figure of the goose-girl is as conventional and delicate as a Dresden shepherdess, not only the look but the gesture – one almost expects her to be standing on a round china base rather than on the ground. The shadow-particles of time dance about her as she looks up at the other-real speaking head of Falada, and the bright and ordinary prettiness of the girl becomes eerie and astonishing: that great shadowy wall is so high, the head of the horse is so powerful in its otherness – how can the girl endure the forces flickering through and around her! For she obviously does endure them, she becomes powerful enough magically and graphically to balance the array of weights and forces. Because each look at the girl is a fresh realisation of that action, the simple composition is kept moving. The effect is heightened if you place the book to one side rather than directly in front of you and let your eyes go out of focus: as your vision shifts in and out of its normal binocular function, the arch of light in the opening of the wall moves back towards the goose-girl and away, back and away; the goose-girl moves into and out of the arch of light, and the geese hurry towards the meadows.

And still that horse's head will not let go of me. I go to the Goethe Institut Library in Princes Gate. There our friends Hanna Tormouche and Luise von Loew bring down thick books from the shelves for me, such treasures as the *Handwörterbuch des Deutschen Aberglaubens (Dictionary of German Superstitions)*. There I find all kinds of things, the words themselves seem to have the shape and timbre of the ideas in them, as: *das Pferd als Führer des Toten*, the horse as guide of the dead. Long and bony and hoof-clopping, those words.

Horses' heads were hung on trees at the shrine of Odin in Uppsala. Horses' heads on poles and fences were used to avert evil. Horses' heads were put on ridgepoles and the gable ends of houses (in Celle in Lower Saxony, where my wife was born, you can still see the barge-boards at the gable ends carried up to crossed horses' heads at the ridge of the roof). Horses' heads in so many times and places! Horses' heads buried under doorsteps; last-sheaf horses' heads; the cut-off head of the 'October Horse' decorated with loaves of bread. And coming back from the Goethe Institut I pass, on the Fulham Road in London, just a few doors from Pan

Books, a horse's head over a gateway at the Hungry Horse Restaurant.

These things whirl in my head, and I find that whirling gyroscopically stabilising. Society relegates to superstition that range of signification that it cannot use in the reality-frame of every day, but reality does not end at the limits of society's frail consensus; the unknowable thingness of things and the ideas that emanate from it are equally real with all things else. Myth and story have the practical function of keeping us in touch with the unknown and unknowable in ourselves and in the universe. The more awareness we have of the other-than-rational in us, the better able we are to be reasonable in our actions.

Goya wrote – I think it was on the title-page of *Los Caprichos* – 'The dream of Reason produces monsters'. I don't think that's how it is. I think it's when reason is *not* allowed to dream that it acts out its dreams while awake, and then it is that monsters are produced, in Goya's time and in ours. Modern scientists studying the phenomena of sleep have found that the person who is prevented from dreaming soon cannot function properly when awake. I believe that both as individuals and as a society we can find a healthy balance only when our minds (or mind) can move freely from the ordinary to the extraordinary reality-frame. The healthy mind knows where it is and draws its sustenance from different realms for dream and waking action. The danger of those fictions current now in television, films, and government is that violent and uncontrollable dreams have moved out of the realm of the extraordinary and into the ordinary, there to become part of our stock of usable action. Our rapists and our hooligans and our armament-racing heads of state are wide awake and going about their ordinary business.

Enough of that. 'The Goose-Girl' has taken me *weit über Feld*. With that one tale my tracing of origins and my metaphysical speculations begin and end. *Household Tales* will happen to you according to how you are and where you are when you read them. With or without detective-work these stories will put you someplace you have never been before; that action is ongoing in them and in you. The best of it is, I think, the tingling of not-knowing and knowing at the same time. Be the youngest simple son or daughter, go into the world and take your chance. Encounter, in a state of not-knowing, whatever comes your way: three wishes, three giants or three labours. Find supernatural helpers, little people, speaking animals or devils; make magical descents to depths where toads give golden rings and talismans. And all the time feel in you the knowing that *if* the trapdoor opens, *if* the helper beckons, *if* the chance should offer, it will not be missed.

At the Goethe Institut Library I borrowed Ruth Michaelis-Jena's *The Brothers Grimm**. If this essay should introduce you to that book as well as this one, my time will have been well spent.

The mother of Jacob and Wilhelm Grimm was born Dorothea Zimmer; their father was Philipp Wilhelm Grimm, town clerk at Hanau. In 1791 he became *Amtmann* (justiciary) of Steinau, a little town in the Kinzig valley. There were five children then, all boys: Jacob was six years old; Wilhelm five; Carl four; Ferdinand three; and Ludwig one. A sister, Charlotte Amalie, was born in 1793.

Ruth Michaelis-Jena tells us:

> The *Amtshaus* ... was a handsome half-timbered building, surrounded by gardens and a walled courtyard. The façade had consoles and rafters, finely carved with scrolls and fantastic figures. One irregular beam ended in a little squinting devil which both fascinated and frightened the children. There were stables and outhouses, a turret stair and a huge lime tree at the front door.

If one were to design the perfect childhood, it would be such

*Routledge & Kegan Paul, 1970.

153

a one as the brothers Grimm enjoyed in Steinau: they had a loving, cheerful mother and a good father who wore 'a blue frock coat, with red velvet collar and gold epaulettes, leather breeches and boots with silver spurs'; there were postilions and horses, foresters and goose-girls; woods and hills and fields; storks and swallows, cows and sheep; festivals and traditions; sowing and reaping and spinning in the natural order of the seasons.

The idyll ended with the death of their father in 1796 but the goodness of that childhood lasted. From the time they first saw the light of day, Jacob and Wilhelm Grimm had found themselves in an abundant world and among people who cared for one another in a network of love and attention and practical detail. No misfortune or later unhappiness could stand up against that. All their lives they remained true and loving to each other and the people and the world around them. They lived in a constant opening up of sense and intellect, a continual deepening of fidelity that animated for them voices scarcely heard and half-forgotten – earth voices whose words and timbre they would labour to preserve. 'The very blood can call and speak . . . ' they said, and they listened.

The brothers Grimm knew well what they were doing, knew the myths that lay behind them, knew these tales' proper place in social and in literary evolution. They worked not for some prettified ideal of childhood but for the ongoing 'What if?' that is humankind. What they did in their work with language and folklore was simply to repay with everything that was in them the life that gave them life and the world that gave them world. With loving care and steadfast labour they gathered and they gleaned as if they themselves were one double avatar of the fruitful corn-spirit, offering with full hands their plenty to us then and now and later.

In the introduction to the first edition of *Household Tales*, published in 1812, Jacob and Wilhelm Grimm wrote:

... when the heavens have unleashed a storm, or when some other natural disaster has battered down a whole harvest, we may well find that in some sheltered corner by the roadside, under hedges and shrubs, a few ears of corn have survived. When the sun begins to shine again, they will grow, hidden and unnoticed. No early scythe will cut them for the corn-houses. Only late in summer, when the ears are ripe and heavy with grain, some poor humble hand will glean them, and bind them carefully, one by one. The little bundles will be carried home, more cherished than big sheaves, and will provide food for the winter, and perhaps the only seed for the future ...

1976

'I, that was a child,
my tongue's use sleeping . . . '

Written for the June 1984 Seminar of the Israel Association of American Studies in Tel Aviv. The theme of the seminar was 'The American Dream'.

Everyone lives a life that is seen and a life that is unseen. Our dreams are part of our unseen life. We often forget our own dreams and we have no idea whatever of the dreams of others: last night the person next to you in the underground may have ridden naked on a lion or travelled under the sea to the lost city of Atlantis. Along with the dream life there is the life of ideas and half-ideas, of glimmerings and flashes and indescribable atmospheres of the mind. What we actually do in what is called the real world depends largely on how we live this unseen life in our inner world of words and images, songs and bits of poems, names and numbers and memories and dreams remembered and unremembered. Whether the song in our heads is Michael Jackson or Franz Schubert it is fitting itself to and reinforcing something in us that comes forward to meet it. That's how art affects life; we use it to be more what we are and to become what is in us wanting us to become it. The world of the song or the poem is met by other worlds known to us or hidden in our dreams.

In dreams one often sees the house of one's childhood. Years and years have passed, one's own children have grown up and gone out into the world; but in dreams the house of

156

childhood is fresh and strong, the smell of its closets, the creak of its floors, the light through its windows and the shadows of leaves – everything resonates in the sleeping mind. Perhaps tonight one will find the lost toy or see more clearly something only half-glimpsed long ago. And perhaps today if I begin with the house of my childhood I can find my way to that unseen part of my life that grows out of and into what is called The American Dream.

The house of my childhood was in Lansdale, Pennsylvania. My parents were Russian Jews from a town in the Ukraine called Ostrog. They're both dead now and my two sisters and I continue their outward journey from that town we've never seen. They were both young when they came to America. My father had been poor in Russia, he told me how once outside a bakery he had seen a boy with a freshly-bought cheese pastry take out the cheese and throw away the crust which he, my father, then picked up and ate. There was in our house a halting little oil painting he had done on a wooden panel: it was a platoon of Russian cavalry, horsemen with slung carbines and bed-rolls, just a little clump of figures on horses, seen from the back. Now I call to mind this picture that I haven't seen for almost fifty years and I have no idea what it was to him.

My mother came to America before my father, in 1911 I think, when she was seventeen. She came with her sisters and she worked as a seamstress to earn my father's passage. He became a newsboy in Philadelphia, he had a dog who sat on the back of his bicycle. He made friends with some of the staff of *The Jewish Daily Forward* who used to buy papers from him. He went to night classes and lectures; I am named after Dr Russell Conwell who gave a famous lecture called 'Acres of Diamonds' in which a man travelled the world in search of wealth and then found it in his own backyard.

My father bought Dr Eliot's Five-Foot Shelf, the Harvard Classics; also E. Haldeman-Julius's Little Blue Books in one of which Dr Emil Coué said that every day in every way he was getting better and better; also Krafft-Ebing's *Psychopathia Sexualis* in which all the best parts were in Latin; also *Sunshine and Health Magazine* in which respectable ladies and gentlemen were shown in respectably drooping nakedness drinking tea and playing tennis.

My father gave me a book, *Fairy Tales for Workers' Children*. I was taught never to cross a picket line and always to eat the union label on loaves of rye and pumpernickel for good luck. My father had become Advertising Manager of *The Jewish Daily Forward* and Director of the Drama Guild of the Labor Institute of the Workmen's Circle of Philadelphia. He directed Yiddish classics and contemporary American plays of social comment such as *Stevedore*, *1931*, and *Can You Hear Their Voices?* Sometimes my sisters and I got onstage; in the play *1931* a jobless man begged a dime from a passer-by who tossed it so that it fell to the ground. I was a newsboy who grabbed the dime. I had one line to speak: 'It's mine, I saw it first!'

My mother raised pigeons, two thousand of them. We had a hired man who helped with the pigeons and our one-acre truck patch. My father's younger brother, my uncle Jack, had a frequently broken-down roadster called Natasha and liked to play baseball. Sometimes I rode in Natasha's rumble seat. On the wall by my bed I had a chromolithographed cardboard display figure of King Kong on top of the Empire State Building with an aeroplane in one hand and Fay Wray in the other. Ethel Waters sang 'Stormy Weather' on the radio and sad-faced men came to the back door and asked if they could do some chores for a meal. My mother fed them and I sat on the porch with them while they ate their share of the American Dream.

One speaks of the American Dream and the meaning varies with the speaker but always what is meant is a montage of heart-pictures, desire-pictures, richly coloured wishes and memories and expectations of what people variously want from America or associate with America. This montage may have in it the Declaration of Independence, John D. Rockefeller, the Ku Klux Klan, Daniel Boone and Joseph McCarthy, Shirley Temple and the mountain men and Charlie Parker; it may have Abe Lincoln and Billy the Kid and the Statue of Liberty lifting her lamp beside the golden door of the Land of Opportunity where the plough breaks the plains, the West is won, the Yanks are coming, the Wright brothers and the astronauts go up and the economy comes down, Henry David Thoreau plants beans at Walden Pond, the Okies roll out of the dustbowl in battered Fords and talking blues by Woody Guthrie, Frank Sinatra sings at Las Vegas, Thomas Wolfe burns in the night and Jack Dempsey, Marilyn Monroe, Diamond Jim Brady, P. T. Barnum and the *Enola Gay* gleam in the high sunlight over Hiroshima while Bartolomeo Vanzetti writes a letter to his son and survivalists in Texas stockpile provisions and machine guns. The American Dream is pretty much whatever montage of heart-pictures you like to look at.

In every montage of heart-pictures lives the house of childhood, the physical one that still stands and perhaps is lived in by strangers or has burnt down or been demolished or stands desolate with broken suitcases and old letters with blurred writing under rotting leaves and broken glass and the rain coming in through empty windows.

There is another house of childhood and this one is of the mind. In my house of childhood of the mind lives Vol. XVII of the Harvard Classics. Vol. XVII was the only book in the Five-Foot Shelf much handled; Locke and Hume and Darwin looked as new as the day they were unpacked but Vol. XVII was *Folklore and Fable*, Andersen and Aesop and the brothers Grimm, and it was in heavy use. Oscar Wilde's *House of Pomegranates* and *The Arabian Nights* live there also. As a child I did much of my reading in the room in our house called the library. It was lined with books in Russian, Yiddish, and

English and had a massive oak table. No one else I knew had such a room. I had outdoor reading places as well, and of these my favourite was a big old wild cherry tree where in season I read *Robin Hood* and ate little sun-warmed black cherries.

This house that childhood builds in the mind is a learning place and a place where we test words and images and ideas to find out what rings true. Also it's like a safe house in a spy film: in it the secret agent that is the child's mind can stay hidden until ready to venture armed into the hostile city. It isn't the world that is hostile – the stone and the leaf and the door of the world beckon and welcome – it's the grey city of the world that threatens, the grey city of the failed children of the world, the dry thinkers, the juiceless minds, the poison skulls that dream in numbers and megadeaths. They run the world, these failed children; they speak in all languages and in all languages their speech is vile. In bemedalled uniforms, in costly business suits and ties they mouth pompous words printed out by grey machines. Each one thinks the other is the enemy while the real enemy, the monster they have called up together, sings to itself outside the window. The grey city is why the safe house of childhood of the mind is needed, and long after the child is grown this safe house is still needed in the shadows and the narrow alleys by the waterfront in the grey city of terror.

This house of childhood is not a foolish place, it is the true place where first recognitions happen all through life; it is the place where I heard for the first time what is in the Beethoven quartets and Bach's *Art of Fugue* and Schubert's *Die Winterreise*; it is where Oedipus made his tragedy belong to him and was no longer a victim, where Conrad's Jim jumped from the *Patna* into lostness, where Rubashov in *Darkness at Noon* accepted one by one the consequences of the ideas he had lived by; it is where I took in unknown pages that came alive years later like water in the desert, it is where T. S. Eliot said, in *Little Gidding*:

> We die with the dying:
> See, they depart, and we go with them.
> We are born with the dead:
> See, they return, and bring us with them.
> The moment of the rose and the moment
>   of the yew-tree
> Are of equal duration.

Since 1969 I've lived in London. I'm a stranger at home under grey English skies and walking by European rivers but I still weapon and provision myself in the house of childhood that was built in America. Are there in that house recognitions that are peculiarly American? Yes, I think so. Here is one:

> Out of the cradle endlessly rocking,
> Out of the mocking-bird's throat, the musical shuttle,
> Out of the Ninth-month midnight,
> Over the sterile sands and the fields beyond, where the
>   child leaving his bed wander'd alone, bareheaded,
>   barefoot,
> Down from the shower'd halo,
> Up from the mystic play of shadows twining and
>   twisting as if they were alive,
> Out from the patches of briers and blackberries,
> From the memories of the bird that chanted to me,
> From your memories sad brother, from the fitful
>   risings and fallings I heard,
> From under that yellow half-moon late-risen and
>   swollen as if with tears ...

In Walt Whitman's magical lyric the poet listens through the night to the 'lone singer wonderful', the mocking-bird, the solitary he-bird who guards the nest and the eggs to which his mate never returns.

Demon or bird! (said the boy's soul),
Is it indeed toward your mate you sing? or is it really to me?
For I, that was a child, my tongue's use sleeping, now
    I have heard you,
Now in a moment I know what I am for, I awake,
And already a thousand singers, a thousand songs, clearer,
    louder and more sorrowful than yours,
A thousand warbling echoes have started to life within
    me, never to die.

In the last part of the poem he asks for a word from the sea:

Whereto answering, the sea,
Delaying not, hurrying not,
Whisper'd me through the night, and very plainly
    before day-break,
Lisp'd to me the low and delicious word death,
And again death, death, death, death,
Hissing melodious, neither like the bird nor like my
    arous'd child's heart,
But edging near as privately for me rustling at my feet,
Creeping thence steadily up to my ears and laving me
    softly all over,
Death, death, death, death, death.

Which I do not forget,
But fuse the song of my dusky demon and brother,
That he sang to me in the moonlight on Paumanok's
    gray beach,
With the thousand responsive songs at random,
My own songs awaked from that hour,
And with them the key, the word up from the waves,
The word of the sweetest song and all songs,
That strong and delicious word which, creeping to my
    feet,
(Or like some old crone rocking the cradle, swathed

in sweet garments, bending aside,)
The sea whisper'd me.

This poem was first published in 1859, and at this distance Whitman seems not so much a man as a manifestation, as if the nature of America and its history generated this voice that must inevitably appear. He seems a kind of lesson, a paradigm, this Walt Whitman who read almost inaudibly to a baffled and not very responsive audience and then wrote the newspaper account of the same reading in which he described himself as filling the auditorium with his booming masculine voice and being interrupted continually by applause; Walt Whitman the non-boomer, the whisperer in the darkness at the heart of the American Dream, driven by his demon to step out from behind his laborious persona for this profound and shadowy rite of passage. Nations have national characteristics: I think that we Americans have both a propensity for bullshit and an inborn drive to cut through the bullshit. (I have to use this word, there isn't any other for what I mean – 'bombast' won't do it.) The wonderfully American thing about this poem is that it took this bullshit artist of the open road and made him write it so that it could become itself. I love that.

'Out of the Cradle Endlessly Rocking' is a hermetic lyric; it is of the realm of Hermes, the whisperer in the darkness, the guide of souls and the god of thieves and roadways and journeys. On the day Hermes was born he invented the lyre and stole the cattle of Apollo. To make the sound-box of the lyre he scooped a living tortoise out of its shell, he killed something to make an emptiness for his music to come out of. Then after making music he was hungry for meat so he stole Apollo's cattle.

Hermes is not officially the god of artists and the arts but he is for me: in some way there is always the killing of something to make that necessary emptiness from which the art comes and in some way the artist is always stealing what he hungers for, stealing cattle that can never be owned, cattle of beauty, cattle of truth and pain, cattle of minutes and hours – as often as not simply stealing that part of himself that is somebody else's cattle, stealing it for a secret life of finding and losing and mystery.

However it came to be there, that emptiness in Whitman wherein he heard the sea and the word from the sea is an American emptiness – you can see it in the heartbreaking summer dusk over the pines and the illuminated globes on the gas pumps in an Edward Hopper painting; you can see it in the faded lettering that says PURINA CHOWS on the side of a deserted Pennsylvania barn. Hopper and Whitman both bring their music out of that emptiness and both of them stole the cattle of themselves out of the herd of not-belonging-to-self.

Hermes is the god of journeys, and that long road that passes Edward Hopper's Maine gas station is the one that America has travelled from its beginning: the spirit of America is a journeying one; everyone in America has always been on the way from one place to another, one condition to another. Our only original music comes from the descendants of slaves on their way from otherness into America's idea of itself. American blues and jazz have always in them the long road and the shining rails dwindling to a point ahead and behind; our characteristic music is always going somewhere, moving, travelling, on that train and gone with long-gone John from Bowling Green, gone with Easy Rider where the Southern meets the Yellow Dog, gone where that Midnight Special shines its light on you and me and the journeying and imprisoned soul of the Land of the Free.

How imprisoned? Like all individuals and like all nations America is a prisoner of its history, of what was done and what was not done. How many dead bodies and dead hopes has the American Dream left behind it in the domestic and foreign venues where it has played? And like all individuals and nations America is a prisoner of its own idea of itself. False legends and tall stories proliferate faster than the truth. Too often we have come blinking out of the cinema of our hopeful vanity and ridden off into the pollution tall in the saddle with John Wayne. What we truly are is a mystery to us; this mystery is continually in the process of finding a voice and for this it used Walt Whitman in his time; it used him to speak the darkness below all history and all legend, the darkness that is not only death but the womb of that mystery out of which comes new becoming.

In his chapter on Hermes in his book, *The Homeric Gods*, Walter F. Otto has this to say about the mother-darkness that is the realm of Hermes:

> A man who is awake in the open field at night or who wanders over silent paths experiences the world differently than by day. Nighness vanishes, and with it distance; everything is equally far and near, close by us and yet mysteriously remote. Space loses its measures. There are whispers and sounds, and we do not know where or what they are. Our feelings too are peculiarly ambiguous. There is a strangeness about what is intimate and dear, and a seductive charm about the frightening. There is no longer a distinction between the lifeless and the living, everything is animate and soulless, vigilant and asleep at once . . . Danger lurks everywhere . . . Who can protect him, guide him aright, give him good counsel? The spirit of Night itself, the genius of its kindliness, its enchantment, its resourcefulness, and its profound wisdom. She is indeed the mother of all mystery.

And a word from the other great Hermes-friend, Karl Kerenyi:

For the great mystery, which remains a mystery even after all our discussing and explaining, is this: the appearance of a speaking figure, the very embodiment as it were in a human-divine form of clear, articulated, play-related and therefore enchanting, language – its appearance in that deep primordial darkness where one expects only animal muteness, wordless silence, or cries of pleasure and pain. Hermes the 'Whisperer' (*psithyristes*) inspirits the warmest animal darkness.

This also from Kerenyi:

What he [Hermes] brings with him from the springs of creation is precisely the 'innocence of becoming'.

For me innocence of becoming is associated with the idea of the unfailed and unfailing child. This follows on my earlier thought of the grey city of failed children. Now I have to say a little more about the unfailed child. In order to do this I must go back in my thinking and my reading to the sources of this idea.

'The overall number of minds is just one,' said Schrödinger. There's no way of proving this; one can only test it against one's own experience. Does consciousness feel like that, as if there's only one mind? To me it does. I feel inhabited by a consciousness that looks out through the eyeholes in my face and this consciousness doesn't seem to have originated with me. I feel like a receiver made for a transmission that was going on long before I arrived.

It feels to me as if the total experience of the universe and every image ever imagined or seen, every word ever written or spoken, every thought ever thought is in this one mind, ceaselessly active. And I believe that whatever is in the one mind is in each of us. That being so, the total experience, not only of humanity but of the universe, is in each one of us in this one mind that is always now.

We are the children of the mystery that inhabits us

and I believe that it wants us to meet it with innocence
of becoming; not to meet it is to be a failed child. Perhaps
there haven't yet been any unfailed children but I think that
all of us have unfailed moments. Whitman was unfailing that
night on the beach; by tuning himself to the bird he entered
innocence of becoming and met the mystery. And something
of the American soul followed him and still follows him into
the wondrous dark of it.

As if to demonstrate that they were two aspects of
the same thing, Walt Whitman and Herman Melville were
both born in the same year, 1819, and died in the same year,
1891. Whitman heard the song of the bird and the word from
the sea on Long Island for which he used the Indian name
Paumanok. Melville hunted his whale with a ship called the
Pequod, the name of an extinct Indian tribe. It was as if each
man wanted the ghosts of the original inhabitants at his back
when the one invoked the savage mother and the other the
white whale.

'Hark ye yet again, – the little lower layer,' says Ahab.
'All visible objects, man, are but as pasteboard masks.
But in each event – in the living act, the undoubted deed
– there, some unknown but still reasoning thing puts forth
the mouldings of its features from behind the unreasoning
mask. If man will strike, strike through the mask! How
can the prisoner reach outside except by thrusting through
the wall? To me the white whale is that wall, shoved near
to me. Sometimes I think there's naught beyond. But 'tis
enough He tasks me; he heaps me; I see in him outra-
geous strength, with an inscrutable malice sinewing it.
That inscrutable thing is chiefly what I hate; and be the
white whale agent, or be the white whale principal, I will
wreak that hate upon him.'

'I have written a wicked book,' said Melville in a letter
to Hawthorne, 'and feel spotless as the lamb.' So far I've
avoided reading any critical analyses of *Moby Dick* and I

hope to continue doing so; still, I can't help wondering how much of Melville there was in Ahab and whether the Melville/Ahab balance changed after the last harpoon was thrown and the harpoon line that connected Ahab to the whale took him to his death.

The man who does battle with the unknown but reasoning thing behind the mask is dragged under by it and his mother-ship sunk. The innocent heathen Queequeg perishes with the others but his unChristian life-buoy coffin saves Ishmael:

> *Buoyed up by that coffin, for almost one whole day and night, I floated on a soft and dirge-like main. The unharming sharks, they glided by as if with padlocks on their mouths; the savage sea-hawks sailed with sheathed beaks.*

The only survivor is neither the God-maddened Ahab nor the simple savage but the civilised mariner who seems to have attained innocence of becoming. I wonder whether Melville was by then more Ishmael than Ahab, whether through his tragic and absurd hero he had purged himself of rage and recognised that his hate was a kind of love and that the duality of which one element was the enemy was in fact a unity where there was no enemy.

Moby Dick was published in 1851; 'Out of the Cradle Endlessly Rocking' wasn't until 1859; perhaps the American child had to shake its fist at the father before it could be soothed by the mother. Certainly it's a continually growing child and it seems not bound for failure, this child loving enough to beg the word of darkness from the sea and bold enough to steer for the monstrous malevolent jaw. A promising child, I think, personified in 1884 by one Huckleberry Finn who, having written the note that will tell Miss Watson the whereabouts of the runaway slave Jim, finds himself pondering the matter:

> I felt good and all washed clean of sin for the first time I had ever felt so in my life, and I knowed I could pray

now. But I didn't do it straight off, but laid the paper down and set there thinking – thinking how good it was all this happened so, and how near I come to being lost and going to hell. And went on thinking. And got to thinking over our trip down the river; and I see Jim before me, all the time, in the day, and in the night-time, sometimes moonlight, sometimes storms, and we a floating along, talking, and singing, and laughing. But somehow I couldn't seem to strike no places to harden me against him; but only the other kind. I'd see him standing my watch on top of his'n, stead of calling me, so I could go on sleeping, and see him how glad he was when I come back out of the fog; and when I come to him again in the swamp, up there where the feud was; and such-like times; and would always call me honey, and pet me, and do everything he could think of for me, and how good he always was; and at last I struck the time I saved him by telling the men we had small-pox aboard, and he was so grateful, and said I was the best friend old Jim ever had in the world, and the *only* one he's got now; and then I happened to look around, and see that paper.

It was a close place. I took it up, and held it in my hand. I was a trembling, because I'd got to decide, forever, betwixt two things, and I knowed it. I studied a minute, sort of holding my breath, and then says to myself:

'All right, then, I'll *go* to hell' – and tore it up.

Huck Finn, standing alone against the authority of the failed-child establishment and refusing to sell his dark brother down the river, is about as unfailed a child as you can find: a child eminently practical and resourceful, cunning enough to survive the grey city of the world, a child in touch with the mystery of being and always in a state of innocently becoming. An American Dream with him in it has a good chance of not being a nightmare.

I said at the outset that I was going to try to find my way to the unseen part of my life that grows into and out of the American Dream. I've done what I could with that. The seen part of my life is my writing and I was late getting started. It wasn't until 1963 that I, that was a child, my tongue's use sleeping, took typewriter in hand and began to put a novel together. Since then I've tried to keep moving on that wavering edgeline where the sea of the mystery meets the strand of the more or less known, leaving my American footprints in the sand where others have walked before me, listening to the word from the waves, sometimes seeing a ghostly spout far off, and hearing always the long and lonesome whistle of the Midnight Special.

1984

With a Choked Cry

'*With a choked cry, the coxwain loosed his grasp upon the shrouds, and plunged head first into the water.*' That was the caption under one of the illustrations in the copy of *Treasure Island* I owned as a boy: Jim Hawkins, looking desperate, perched in the mizzen cross-trees of the *Hispaniola*, firing both his pistols as Israel Hands's dirk pins him to the mast. I haven't got the book now and I'm not sure of the name of the illustrator — I think it may have been Reade. I seem to remember a frontispiece in colour, Long John Silver with his parrot, but the rest of the illustrations were pen and ink. Reade (if indeed that was his name) drew with a Romanesquely reiterative line: if a form was worth going around once he went around it two or three times — not sketchily but insistently, like a dog with a bone — and each time the line went round it put a few pounds on whatever it delineated; his people, consequently, had somewhat haggard faces, a lot of wrinkles in their clothes, and they all walked with a heavy tread. When Hands hit the water he would have made a pretty big splash. I haven't seen those drawings for forty-eight years and I can't recall every one but the *look* of them is vivid in my mind and brings back the cosiness, the delight, the sheer well-being I felt when I first read that book, sitting in our wild cherry tree in the summer when I was ten.

Years later we lived in a building that had an incinerator chute on each floor. In the hall there was a metal flap in the wall that let out a current of warm air and the smell of burning when you opened it. In March 1943, just before I left for the army, I opened that flap and down the chute went *Treasure Island, Robin Hood, The Arabian Nights*, and some lesser favourites, all books that I loved and had read several times. I was eighteen and going off to the war, maybe I wasn't coming back; I was presiding over the death of my childhood so I burned those books and when I got to the induction centre I gave my civilian clothes to the Red Cross.

The books that underwent this enforced suttee were all illustrated ones and of course I've been looking for those same editions ever since I came back from the war and found that my early years and I were still alive. The only one that I was able to replace was *Robin Hood*, illustrated by Edwin John Prittie: twenty pictures, four in colour, looking as good as in my childhood, with the people in them, as before, a little better-looking and a little more elegant in gesture and action than one sees in real life. Pictured on the board cover is that first meeting on the narrow bridge when John Little (not yet Little John) knocks Robin into the stream with his quarter-staff. I hold the book in my hand and I can almost feel it hum with the hours of contentment I spent in the company of its departed brother.

My thrown-away *Arabian Nights* was a wonderful job of bookmaking of a much freer kind than *Treasure Island* or *Robin Hood*. The illustrations were all brush and ink by an unforgettably exuberant draughtsman whose name has vanished from my mind; wild they were, every one, and rumbustious with life – some were full-page, some were vignettes, some took up part of a page and the type ran around them. They were all over the book, as if they'd been waiting behind the printed words and had burst out when they couldn't hold themselves back any longer. The blacks of those black-and-white drawings were black like anything, the line was ragged and splotchy, the style was bold and loose and everything was well beyond the ordinary — when the people on those pages saw something that surprised them their eyes nearly jumped out of their heads; when they howled with rage you could hear it for miles; when Sinbad tied himself to the leg of the roc you could see by the terror in his face and the look of that leg (the rest of the bird was off the page) that he was in for a really scary ride. As I recall those drawings now they come with the shouts and background noise of oriental bazaars, the bass rumblings of genies loosed from jugs and lamps, the sweet voices of veiled women, the cries and curses of heroes and villains in strange and violent encounters, and all the sound effects required by the astonishing action of the stories. I've read somewhere of a Chinese or Japanese god of ink, and those drawings were certainly blessed by that god. The paper was coarse and thick, the ink lived in it with a strong life. That book was a treasure, my thrown-away *Arabian Nights*, gone for ever.

Ink on paper makes books; books make worlds. You don't need a printing press, you don't even need to be grown-up. Little children take pieces of paper, of different sizes as often as not; on them they print great gangling words with capitals and lower-case letters not always in the usual places; they draw pictures on the pieces of paper and they staple them together and the pages turn and it's a book with monsters and spacecraft from beyond the galaxy. Or trees and flowers and there was a princess who lived in a castle.

Making books with pictures is a natural function of the human animal — we need them because the world in our eyes is not enough, it has to be imaged in other ways and other styles, it has to be brought into the what-iffery of the mind where everything is more so and where anything can happen. Illustrated books for children help to furnish the mind and improve the critical faculty; they help lookers become perceivers – most of all they simply give more world to the reader all through life.

One of the books I didn't throw away is the Lakeside Press edition of *Moby Dick* illustrated by Rockwell Kent whose drawings, together with the typography and layout, rank with Doré's *Don Quixote*. I lusted after that book and I finally got it for my fourteenth or fifteenth birthday. I knew from the first moment I held it in my hands that we were going to be friends for life. I haven't tried to put into words until now what Kent's austere and passionate evocations of Melville's metaphysics do: what those drawings do, what the best book illustration always does, is to take the mind to a special and peculiar place where mystery lives and words can't go, then return it to the word place sensitised, responsive, and newly perceptive of the world.

1991

North

There is a north in the mind where the white wind blows, where the white ones live. Where the ice bear walks alone, the ice bear swinging his head on his thick neck that is like a great white snake in the body of a bear. Where the white wolf comes trotting, trotting on the paths of the living, the paths of the dead. Where the snowy owl glides in silence through the twilight. Where the raven speaks its word of black. The north where one goes in fear, the north that the compass cannot find, the north that is the cold and implacable truth from which one doesn't always return.

I have never been to the Arctic, never actually seen the wind blowing the snow like smoke off the frozen tundra. The ice bear, the snowy owl, the white wolf and the raven come to me as moving photographic images invisibly transmitted through the air to the television screen where I see them great, mysterious, mythological. North-in-Itself moves in them, it puts on their shapes and shows itself to me in this way. It can do that – having manifested itself to the lens of a camera it can be transported as the seeing of itself retained in an emulsion on a strip of cellulose because the north exists beyond the limits of geography and physical laws; on the compass it is at the same time the 360 degrees of the full circle and Zero, unfindable, unknowable, nothing to be measured.

KINGDOM OF THE ICE BEAR, say the letters on the screen, and the north is activated in the phosphors coating the glass: the ice bear; the beluga whale; ice floes; the walrus; caribou stags fighting; the snowy owl, a speckled female, her wings backlit, comes in dark against the light from the sea. From a distance her eyes have a dark and frowning shape; with her black beak they give her face a look of command. She brakes with outstretched wings and swings her body down from the horizontal; I see the naked brood patch in her breast-feathers as her legs, reaching for the ground, become very long. The length of her body and legs is surprising, she seems not so much a bird as a magical two-legged winged being, a feathered woman with a face of dreams. How beautiful and strange she is, strange even to herself perhaps; how suddenly not to be denied is the mystery of her in its roundness, its whiteness, its bulk. In my mind the smell of her is sharp as she settles down on her nest with her children, folds her wings and becomes sculptural, a sphinx-bird. Out of the two round windows set deep in the thick feathers of her face she looks at me, and from her luminous golden eyes with a black disc at the centre looks North-in-Itself; it has put on this shape to let itself be seen.

The ice bear appears again, a solitary male swinging his head as he walks the whiteness of himself over the whiteness of snow and ice. I know that he smells of the sea. He is alone in an immensity of emptiness but I think he cannot know what it is to be alone – he himself is the concentrated shape and substance of an aloneness like that of the sea or the sky, a white cosmos of solitude without yearning. I am convinced of this even though I know that he is aware of himself as distinct from the ice and snow: when he stalks a seal he covers his black nose with his paw. To think of him I close my eyes and cover my face with my hands. In the blackness I see a moving luminous blue-green, not in the shape of the bear but like some ancient unknown writing. It is the all-alone word of the walking of the ice bear.

Wait, says the north invisibly travelling through the night

to the phosphors on the glass screen, I want to show you something else. Look, here are the barnacle geese. They feed on grass but they nest on narrow ledges high up on the face of a 100-metre cliff. Between the bottom of the cliff and the valley where they feed is a 300-metre stretch of rock scree. When the goslings are hatched there is no food for them until they reach the valley. Here they are on the first day of their lives standing on the narrow ledge. They cannot wait until they can fly, they must make the descent before they starve.

The elegant black-and-white parents go to the edge of the nesting ledge and flutter down. Now the four little fuzzy day-old children one by one step into the grey air.

Down they plummet, rebounding from the unforgiving buttresses of the cliff to the rocks below. All four of the goslings of this family survive. Others die broken on the rocks or are crippled by the fall and taken by foxes. Some who survive the drop blunder into crevices in the scree and die there slowly. Only the lucky ones reach the grassy valley and the safety of the water.

You see? says the north. I put on these shapes and I do what I do.

You're far away, I say. I'll never go to the north.

Everything has its north, says the north. I'll come to you.

1989

Blighter's Rock

You'll notice that I don't call it by its right name. Speaking its name might not actually bring it on but why take foolish chances. I'm talking about a certain sort of stoppage or ungoing, not infrequently an ongoing ungoing, that sometimes afflicts those whose trade is the writing of fiction. One of the strange truths about fiction is that a practitioner writing with no difficulty on Monday may be utterly incapable of doing it on Tuesday. The poor blighter is suddenly rocked. 'How's it going?' one's friends ask cheerfully. 'It's not,' one replies.

Can you pick it up from casual liaisons? Yes. From toilet seats? Yes. From reading the Sunday supplements? Watching *The South Bank Show*? Yes, yes. There are more ways of picking it up than not.

Various writers deal with it in various ways; alcohol and frequent snacks, the traditional folk-remedies, do little to relieve the blankness of the page. Jogging has been known to result in the odd paragraph and a fair number of heart attacks. Hot baths and cold showers, travel, and other forms of escape are unproductive.

One of the earliest symptoms is a growing dread of blank paper, and at this stage preventative action may still have some effect; certainly, in the mind-to-paper process, one's choice of paper is important. I always use 80-gram yellow A4; it's the kind of yellow the paper manufacturers call gold, and gold is what one is trying to refine the base metal of one's thought into, isn't it. While at the same time making a modest living if possible. Yellow paper definitely has less word resistance than blue; yellow-paper molecules are happier with black-ink molecules than blue-paper ones are, and more susceptible to Brownian or even purpureal motion. I never use white paper – to intensify the blankness of a blank sheet by using white paper is to run to meet trouble considerably more than halfway.

80-gram is the weight and A4 the size I prefer because four is a number associated with Hermes, which name, according to the *Oxford Classical Dictionary*, 'signifies the daemon who haunts or occupies a heap of stones, or perhaps a stone, set up by the roadside for some magical purpose'. I am haunted by that daemon – my desk is littered with stones and I often handle them to feel the dance in the stone which is magic enough for me and will perhaps find its way on to the A4 paper with a little help from Hermes the god of roadways, night journeys, chance, merchants, thieves, and writers who need all the help they can get on their night journeys through the blankness of paper.

Why should a blank sheet of paper be frightening? Well, you never know what's going to find its way on to it, do you. H. P. Lovecraft said, in the very first line of his story, 'The Call of Cthulhu':

The most merciful thing in the world, I think, is the inability of the human mind to correlate all its contents.

Even scattered bits of the mind's contents are scary enough; consider the piece of paper that was blank until there appeared on it:

$$E = mc^2$$

What mind generated that equation? Einstein got it on to paper but was Einstein's mind his alone? Is there an individual mind for each one of us? Is the blankness of the paper an individual blankness for every writer or is there one blankness that waits to swallow everybody? I think that mind is a consciousness not confined to the individual brain but shared by all of us; the brain is the organ that limits that consciousness so that we can carry on the business of every day in the consensual state we call reality. I think much, if not most, of the brain's function is repressive, holding back the accumulated contents of the mind as a dam holds back water, and only allowing such flow as will power those practical systems that get us through the day. If the dam ever broke we should drown in the vast chaotic roar of a flood that would sweep away our limited-reality consensus like a chicken coop.

I know that the mind is ancient. We are descended from the dust of stars, and the mind is more ancient than the stars: the whole history of the universe is in it, and more. The limited-reality consensus ignores the strangeness of our being and the strangeness of the consciousness that lives in us; it maintains a pretence of reasonable thought and action for reasonable objectives. With those thoughts and actions we have achieved the world we find ourselves in now. Goya in his etchings showed us the monsters let loose by the dream of Reason: but Reason, in our time, wide awake and staring, has gone a good way beyond anything that Goya or even Goya and Lovecraft together ever could have imagined.

We have an appetite for terror. We amuse ourselves with horror films and horror stories; the idea of Lovecraft's monstrous dead Cthulhu waiting to come alive in his stone city of R'lyeh beneath the sea is not strange to us – there are receptors in the brain waiting for the neurotransmission of such ideas. Stephen King, whose chunky horrors reliably give good value, may well outsell every other writer on this planet; and video shops everywhere are knee-deep in the unspeakable from beyond the grave, the galaxy, and any boundaries of taste. The immensely successful film *A*

Nightmare on Elm Street has gone into three sequels and the marketing of *Nightmare* toys: Muriel Gray reports, on Channel 4's *Media Show*, that Fred Kreuger, the film's knife-digited and dream-stalking revenant, is now available as 'a cuddly little Freddy Christmas-tree toy'. The possibility that child-killer Freddy will displace the teddy bear on the pillows of young phobophiles to help them make it through the night cannot be ruled out.

A Nightmare on Elm Street was written and directed by Wes Craven, and is impressive in that its impact comes not from its special effects and nasty makeup but from a really scary idea: Fred Kreuger's intended victims dare not sleep because dreams are the channel by which he enters reality. In what appears to be their final confrontation the girl whom Kreuger has been trying to kill seems to defeat him by a negative cathexis:

> NANCY: I take back every bit of energy I gave you. You're nothing. You're shit.

> KREUGER: (*Dematerialising*) Aaaaaaaaah!

At that point, however, there is still more to come. The end, which I shall not reveal, leaves us with no clear distinction between nightmare and waking, no place of safety whatever, and the very nature of reality in question. Millions of filmgoers, and I as well, found that entertaining. Perhaps we even felt at home with it. Why is that? Rilke, in the first of his Duino elegies, said:

> Beauty is nothing but the beginning of terror . . .

There is indeed such a spectrum: look at Vermeer's *Head of a Young Girl* for example – there are reproductions of it everywhere; if you follow your mind into the look with which that girl looks out at you, you come to Thing-in-Itself and the terror at the back of her eyes. You come to what waits in the blank paper: the ungraspable isness of what is. In trying to take hold of it the mind finds only the incomprehensibility of itself and the original terror of Creation, the bursting into being of something out of nothing. And yet the mind – this one mind that we all share – is hungry for that terror.

In the original terror is the vital energy that is the beginning of beauty and everything else – perhaps even a better understanding of the human situation. When it comes at you out of the blank paper it's difficult to sort out what wants to be put into words and it isn't always possible to look straight at it; that's why any blighter can find himself or herself rocked from time to time. But with patience, blank paper of the right kind, and a favouring road from Hermes, one gets unrocked often enough to make it worth the bother.

1989

The Bear in Max Ernst's Bedroom
or The Magic Wallet

Keynote address for the Sixth Annual Literary Conference of the Manitoba Writers' Guild in 1987.

The symbol of the Manitoba Writers' Conference is the Fool of the Tarot deck conceived by Arthur Edward Waite and drawn by Pamela Colman Smith. To begin with we might well have a look at Waite's own *Pictorial Key to the Tarot.* The Fool's card is unnumbered, it is designated Zero, and Waite says of it:

> With light step, as if earth and its trammels had little power to restrain him, a young man in gorgeous vestments pauses at the brink of a precipice among the great heights of the world; he surveys the blue distance before him – its expanse of sky rather than the prospect below. His act of eager walking is still indicated, though he is stationary at the given moment . . .

There at the brink of the precipice but not stepping over the edge I'm going to leave the Fool for the present; I'll come back to him later but first I'd like to fool around with various thoughts that, taking advantage of this chance at an audience, have thrust themselves forward.

In H. P. Lovecraft's novel, *The Case of Charles Dexter Ward,* there appears a letter written by one Jedediah Orne to Joseph Curwen who was doing some really exciting things in his basement workshop. In it Orne says to

183

Curwen:

> I say to you againe, doe not call up Any that you cannot
> put downe; by the which I meane, Any that can in turn
> call up somewhat against you, whereby your powerfullest
> devices may not be of use. Ask of the Lesser, lest the
> Greater shall not wish to Answer, and shall commande
> more than you.

Joseph Curwen and his descendant Charles Dexter Ward
called up entities and forces that threatened to destroy not
only the world but the solar system and the entire universe.
The book is a deliciously cosy read, offering such handy
calling-up formulae as:

Y'AI 'NG'NGAH,

YOG-SOTHOTH

H'EE - L'GEB

F'AI THRODOG

UAAAH

Even on the printed page the words reek of horror; saying
them in the circle of the lamplight on a winter's evening
is a real pleasure. After all, it's only fiction. Just imagine
living in a world in which people called up that which
they could not put down. It scarcely bears thinking of,
does it?

We know what fiction is but it isn't all that easy to
know what reality is. What we call reality doesn't seem
to be the same for everybody; it doesn't even always stay
the same for one person. What's real? Is reality a matter
of choice? Maybe you're eating a little something, a little
pastrami on rye with french fries on the side, and maybe
later you pick up some Chinese takeaway and a couple of
missile bases, maybe one or two long-range nuclear-missile
submarines, and you say to yourself, 'Cholesterol isn't really
real. Nuclear missiles aren't really real.' And everything's all
right for a while but all of a sudden you're in a strange bed

with a nurse standing in front of you all crisp and fresh and
smelling nice and the nurse says, 'Well, Mr Schlemiel, now
you've got to shave all down the front of you because they'll
be doing your bypass operation first thing in the morning.'
And while you're shaving very carefully all down the front
of you somebody else's long-range nuclear missile drops in
and says, 'Let's boogie.'

'Just a moment, please,' you say. 'This isn't real. I'm
not accepting this as reality.'

Nevertheless as you stand there with nothing left of you
but a white shadow burned into a wall you must admit,
however grudgingly, that reality might quite possibly not
be a matter of choice, that it might be there whether you
look at it or not. But it's not only cholesterol and nuclear
missiles that can make trouble – there are all kinds of
things that have no name and can't be described, really
scary dreadful things that live in the mind and maybe you
say, 'They're only in my mind.' Then suddenly you find
that you yourself are in your mind with them and there's
no escape.

'O God! How did I get into my mind! Please, please
let me out!'

And God smiles and says, 'Sorry, your mind is the only
place there is.'

And perhaps you say, 'I don't believe that. What about
Borneo? What about the headwaters of the Amazon? What
about the New York Hilton?'

And God says, 'Go where you like, it's still your mind
that you live in.'

'But God, all these really scary dreadful things in my
mind, surely they aren't real.'

And God says, 'Whatever is, is real.'

'Go on, what about all those horrible nasty thingies
that Joseph Curwen and Charles Dexter Ward called up,
Yog-Sothoth and that lot?'

And God says, 'Look around you.'

Because Yog-Sothoth and any other unwelcome dropper-in you can think of is here. If it wasn't you that called them up then somebody else did – it doesn't matter really, we're all in this together, offering in our various fashions on our various altars. An altar doesn't have to be a piece of furniture – any special field of attention is an altar. The big CERN particle accelerator at Geneva is an altar, the Pentagon is an altar, drawing boards and computer screens all over the world are altars, the brain itself is an altar, and on it are offered the thoughts and wishes that call up what cannot be put down, gods and demons and unnamable presences hungry for their moment, and every single one of them real.

At this point people sometimes stop me and say, 'Hang on, are you saying that these gods and demons actually have an independent reality outside your mind?'

And I say, 'You can't speak of a reality independent of the mind, the mind is the only perceiver of reality there is. We all belong to one mind and everything that's ever happened or been thought of since the beginning of the universe is in that mind and it's all real. I can't always get to it and if I do I can't always put a name to it but it's all there and it's all real: the chair is in my mind and it's real; the table is in my mind and it's real, the birth and death of this universe and other universes are in my mind and they're real. And the great blubbering blue fnergl is in my mind and that's real too.'

'Aha!' says my questioner. 'The great blubbering blue fnergl may be real to you but it isn't real to me.'

And I say, 'Not only is it real but you're standing neck-deep in fnergl shit at this very moment and you refuse to take any notice of it.'

That's where the questioner and I usually walk away in opposite directions shaking our heads.

I've always found reality a risky business but different people deal with it in different ways. One drizzly November evening, I think it was in 1958, I was at the Five Spot in Cooper Square in New York City. Ornette Coleman was playing that night; his altar was his saxophone and he was offering. His music was strange, squawky, Proustian, elliptical, he called up a dark and smoky tohu bohu, a kind of friendly chaos in which his musical sentences trailed off into three dots, disappeared round the dark side of the moon, and came back, renewed like the corn god in the spring, to the immense relief of all of us listening. We hadn't been sure they ever *would* come back but here they were again and we clapped like anything.

In a break between sets I saw Don Cherry nearby, he'd been playing a pocket trumpet, and I said to him – it isn't something I'd say now but I said it then – 'I like the way you're taking risks with your music.'

He looked at me in a certain way, then he said, 'Man, we ain't taking no risks – however we're blowing, that's how we're blowing tonight.'

I staggered back, annihilated. It was as if he had taken the Protestant work ethic and broken it across his knee like a cheap fiddle. 'That's how we're blowing tonight.' There are many ways to blow and one is as good as another and that's how we're blowing tonight. Well, I thought, there it is: The Decline of the West, anything goes, no more standards and everyone can do as he likes.

I liked the music but I didn't know how to deal with the world-view apparently expressed by the words. I pondered those words over and over and I never could quite get my head around them. Risk-taking was a big thing in my mind at the time. Only a year before that I'd left my TV art director job at J. Walter Thompson to become a freelance illustrator. That was a risk I'd hesitated to take: I had a wife and three children and a mortgage, I was a responsible citizen with a lot to lose. One evening coming home on the train I'd said to my friend Harvey Cushman, who worked at another advertising agency, 'When I have

$10,000 in the bank and a couple of steady accounts I'll do it.'

'You'll never do it then,' said Harvey. 'I've heard lots of guys say the same thing and somehow the time never comes. If you're going to do it you'll do it without the $10,000 and the steady accounts.'

So I did it and I prospered and I was confirmed in my belief that the human animal is a hunting and finding and risk-taking animal. Finding work was a risk-taking thing and so was doing the work: there were safe ways and dangerous ways of going at a job of illustration and the dangerous ways might result in time and money lost and the work rejected. What defines risk, after all? Risk is when you have something to lose.

When I said that Ornette Coleman was taking risks what did I think he risked losing? Music that worked artistically, music that was a successful product. Now thirty years later I think that Ornette Coleman and his colleagues weren't blowing product, product was no part of their blowing. I think they were blowing process; they were blowing this is where we are at this moment, they were blowing the long dark and the wandering night, they were blowing find it and lose it and keep moving and find it again. Or something else. Or not. They were blowing metaphysical rambling shoes and quantum physics midnight specials and the uncertainty principle. Process, not product. No product to lose, no risk. Only the process of being and unbeing. Many worlds, and this is the one we're blowing tonight. I saw a film about Ornette Coleman recently. In it he recalled hearing some Nigerian musicians when he visited Africa: 'I said, "I gotta go and play with these guys," because I could see that for once I would be able to play whatever passed through my heart and head without ever having to worry about was it right or wrong.'

That's how it is for Ornette Coleman. Is it like that for a writer? Certainly when you've got to where you know how not to get in your own way you can tune in to things and write whatever passes through your heart and head without having to worry about whether it's right or wrong. The process itself becomes the product, and are there then no risks?

Well, here I can only speak from my own experience. I find that in order to tune in to things I have to spend about ten hours a day at my desk. I have to stay up late and let the night into me so that the bricks of reason move apart and the other comes in through the cracks. The electric light changed a lot of things. It was an Irish writer, maybe Padraic Colum but I'm not sure, who said that traditional story-telling had to do with the circle of the firelight and the night all round. When electricity banished the night something was lost. So you have to let the night back in because it's the mother and the mother is where everything comes from. You have to let the night back in and you have to listen to what wants to speak to you. Maybe sometimes you even have to call up what can't be put down, you have to talk to demons and horrors private and public; you must remember that all of us collectively have called up what can't be put down, we have pre-empted Armageddon and it wants to be talked to in the night, it has many things to tell us, many things to whisper and shout and shriek in the silence of the night. Sometimes the voice is that of Beelzebub, sometimes that of Eurydice.

The writer has to listen to those voices because the straight people seem not to have the capability of living in full reality. The straight people live in a limited-reality consensus in which the chair is real, the table is real, the aeroplane is real, the summit meeting is real, but what is inexplicable and ungraspable and nameless isn't real. So the writer has to find names and handles, the writer has to find words to make it real. And yes, there are some risks: you might ruin your health or your wife or husband might leave you or you might write yourself beyond the point of no return and get altogether lost in the dark. But if that's your thing you have to do it. Don't do it if you can stand not doing it, but if you can't stand not doing it, then do it. Because there's so much that needs tuning in to. Why are we what we are? And before you can ask that question, *what* is it that we are? Why do we have some of the thoughts we have? When I find myself standing on top of a tall building or on the edge of a cliff why do I have the urge to throw myself off? Our Fool who pauses so grandly on the brink, does he possibly have that urge? Has anybody else in this room ever had it? I'll be very surprised if I don't see a fair number of hands. Is that urge included in the limited-reality consensus? When Reagan sits down with Gorbachev does Reagan's interpreter say to Gorbachev's interpreter, 'Tell me, Mikhail, when you stand on the edge of a cliff do you have an urge to throw yourself off?' And does Gorbachev's interpreter reply, 'Funny you should mention that, Ron, because I do have that very urge. Do you?' And does Reagan's interpreter say, 'Yes, as a matter of fact I do'? And does Gorbachev's interpreter then say, 'Maybe we're all a little bit crazy, do you think? Maybe there's a craziness in the human situation?'

I doubt that they talk about those things. But the reality of it is that all of us are more than a little bit crazy and there is indeed a craziness in the human situation. The ancient Greeks put a name to that craziness, they called it Dionysus, and having given it a name they could take it into account. At the Pentagon I don't suppose they talk about Dionysus very much but they do have a strategy called Mutual Assured Destruction, of which the acronym is MAD. If it's mad why have they got such a plan, you may well ask. They've got it because there is a madness that lives us, even the Very Important People in the Pentagon and the Kremlin. The following is from *Dionysus, Myth and Cult*, by the religious historian Walter F. Otto:

The elemental depths gape open and out of them a monstrous creature raises its head before which all the limits that the normal day has set must disappear. There man stands on the threshold of madness – in fact, he is already part of it even if his wildness which wishes to pass on into destructiveness still remains mercifully hidden. He has already been thrust out of everything secure, everything settled, out of every haven of thought and feeling, and has been flung into the primeval cosmic turmoil in which life, surrounded and intoxicated with death, undergoes eternal change and renewal.

But the god himself is not merely touched and seized by the ghostly spirit of the abyss. He, himself, is the monstrous creature which lives in its depths. From its mask it looks out at man and sends him reeling with the ambiguity of nearness and remoteness, of life and death in one.

What Otto is saying, what I'm saying, is that it's a strange and frightening thing to be a human being, to partake of the mystery and the madness of human consciousness. Listen to what George Steiner says in his book *The Death of Tragedy*:

Tragic drama tells us that the spheres of reason, order and justice are terribly limited and that no progress in our science or technical resources will enlarge their relevance. Outside and within man is *l'autre*, the 'otherness' of the world. Call it what you will: a hidden or malevolent God, blind fate, the solicitations of hell, or the brute fury of our animal blood. It waits for us in ambush at the crossroads. It mocks us and destroys us. In certain rare instances, it leads us after destruction to some incomprehensible repose.

Dionysus and 'the other' are outside us and within us. So is Hermes, the Priapic god, the thief-god, the god of roadways and night journeys, of chance and change and all kinds of shadowy connections. Here I quote myself, from *The Medusa Frequency*:

Hermes is a mode of event, a shift in the relativities of the moment, a new disposition of energies. There's what you might call a frequency of probability when complementary equivalents offer and anything can be anything.

The nice thing about Hermes is that it likes change, it enjoys alternative universes in which alternative people do alternative things like not destroying themselves. Our Fool on the brink has a strong Dionysiac element in him but he's got a lot of Hermes as well – our Fool is a wender of many ways who always finds new ways, a chance-taker who finds new chances.

Dionysus and the other and Hermes account for some of the action that keeps us popping like popcorn in a popper but there's no end to it, really, and no end to the names and words that need to be found to provide handles for it, and all of the names and words are out in the real reality beyond the limited-reality consensus. We haven't got a lot of time, the world is being destroyed by people to whom hairspray is real but the ozone layer is not, so they kill the whales to feed the dogs and cats; people for whom the sea is not real so they fill it with poisons and garbage; people for whom the rain forests are not real so they cut them down and put in European-style farms that fail. The survival of the human race depends on a realer grasp of reality than we've been capable of so far. The survival of the human race depends on recognising what lives in the human mind and learning how not to be annihilated by it.

There have been attempts in the arts to go further and deeper than the limited-reality consensus. There was dada. In Europe it began in Zurich in 1916. 'The dadaists', says H. H. Arnason in his *History of Modern Art*, 'felt that reason and logic had led to the disaster of world war, and that the only way to salvation was through political anarchy, the natural emotions, the intuitive and the irrational.'

New York dada had begun earlier, in 1913, and later the American and European movements merged. The dadaists were out to produce anti-art art, and they did it in every way they could. In addition to anti-art drawings and paintings in the traditional media they made anti-art art out of snippets from newspapers, bits of photographs and fabrics, and unlikely objects of all kinds, the less artistic the better – a urinal was featured in one exhibition. Marcel Duchamp did a now-famous drawing titled *The Bride Stripped Bare by Her Bachelors, Even*. It looks as if it came from the desk of a physicist or a mathematician or a mechanic; the shapes and ciphers have at first glance nothing to do with brides, bachelors, or stripping bare.

All sorts of reasons can be brought forward to account for dada and I'm sure they're all perfectly valid. It was a time of disillusion and cynicism and disgust with all established authority both political and artistic. But all of the reasons for it add up to one reason: the reality consensus of the time was incapable of dealing with the realities of the time so it had to be expanded. Everything that went into dada, all the snippets and bits of all kinds of things, all the imagery of shock and surprise, of paradox and unreason, all of that is really only part of the ambient uproar that goes on in anybody's head at any time, even when stripping the bride bare. To the contemporary mind, continually bombarded as it is by high-velocity data of unlimited variety, dada oughtn't to be surprising and it no longer is.

The art world applied itself diligently to the further expansion of the reality consensus: surrealism followed hard on dada's heels with Dali's soft watches and Magritte's strange castle-bearing planetoid rock that hovers forever over a grey sea. André Breton said that the purpose of surrealism was 'to resolve the previously contradictory conditions of dream and reality into an absolute reality, a super-reality'. By now surrealism has been absorbed into realism along with Sigmund Freud and our wildest dreams; what was strange has become familiar, and the familiar in strange contexts no longer startles us.

The dadaists and the surrealists wrote a great many manifestos but no novels that I know of. The fictional opening-up of acknowledged reality jolted forward with a great bump when Sylvia Beach published James Joyce's *Ulysses* in 1922. I feel that I ought to say something about this book but the fact is that when I tried to read it at the age of seventeen I found Buck Mulligan and Stephen Dedalus dead boring and I never got beyond the first chapter. Having another go at my present age of sixty-two I found them freshly boring and got no further than the first time. I accept that the book is a literary landmark and I move on to the bear in Max Ernst's bedroom.

This bear lives in a collage done by Ernst around 1920 with gouache and pencil. The picture is a straight-ahead perspective of a long room with a floor of bare boards. The walls are bare except for an indistinct picture on the wall to the right. By the back wall Ernst has glued on a sheep and a bear. These and the other animals and objects in the room all seem to have been cut out of some old schoolbook. Towards the right foreground are a dining-table, a bed, and a wardrobe. In the left foreground a brown-coloured whale swims through the floorboards near a bat and a fish and a coiled snake. The right wall is a sickly grey-green; the rear wall is a pinkish grey; the left wall is pale greenish-grey. The floor is grey with great blotches that look like tear stains. Above the picture is written a caption in German, below it the same caption in French: *Max Ernst's bedroom – it is worth spending a night in it.*

'One might define a collage', said Ernst, 'as an alchemical composite of two or more heterogeneous elements, resulting from their unexpected conjunction, due either to a will orientated – for the sake of clarity – towards a systematic confusion and the disordering of the senses or to pure chance, or perhaps to a will favouring chance.'

I showed my nine-year-old son Wieland a reproduction of *Max Ernst's bedroom* and asked him what he thought of it. 'It's very nice,' he said. 'I like it when the different parts of a picture don't have anything to do with each other.' Wieland is comfortable with the alchemy of that particular collage, I'm not. For me there's something so very bleak, so very dismal and dreary in that room. It's some kind of a paradigm of an aspect of things I'd rather not know about but how can I not know when it's in my mind? Maybe it's the shape of the room or the greyness and the greenness; maybe it's the eyes of the bear, they look as if something's been done to them, as if the bear might have been blinded. Nobody knows the shape of this universe or the shapes of the many possible other universes, nobody knows the infinite regress of that bear into the distances and the depths of the mind perceiving it. I was in hospital recently for heart surgery, and while recovering I was on five or six different drugs, some of which made me dream repetitive dreams of a dismal and tedious character. Obviously there had to be a place in my mind for those dreams to come from, and it's to that place that Max Ernst's bedroom takes me. I think I must have spent many nights in that room, and when I'm there I suppose I'm glued on the same as the sheep and the bear. Perhaps one morning the paper bear will have a bulging belly and I'll be just a few glued-on paper bones and scraps on that tear-blotched floor.

There are many such places in the mind, places of bleakness and horror and despair. How could there not be? Look at our history. There are also places beyond bleakness and horror and despair, places where there is neither reason nor fear, where there is only the sea of whatever is, and the swimmer swimming in that sea. These places are beyond all known edges and off all charts, they must be found again and again and claimed and named by the mind that goes in fear and trembling, but goes to where its being takes it.

Now let's come back to Waite's words about the Fool whom we left on the brink of the precipice:

His act of eager walking is still indicated, though he is stationary at the given moment; his dog is still bounding. The edge which opens on the depth has no terror; it is as if angels were waiting to uphold him if it came about that he leaped from the height. His countenance is full of intelligence and expectant dream. He has a rose in one hand and in the other a costly wand, from which depends over his right shoulder a wallet curiously embroidered. He is a prince of the other world on his travels through this one – all amidst the morning glory, in the keen air. The sun, which shines behind him, knows whence he came, whither he is going, and how he will return by another path after many days. He is the spirit in search of experience. Many symbols of the Instituted Mysteries are summarised in this card, which reverses, under high warrants, all the confusions that have preceded it ... I will give these further indications regarding the Fool, which is the most speaking of all symbols. He signifies the journey outward, the state of the first emanation, the graces and passivity of the spirit. His wallet is inscribed with dim signs, to show that many subconscious memories are stored up in the soul.

I must say that this Waite/Smith fool seems a bit of a *poseur* to me. I prefer French and Italian versions of this card in which the Fool is altogether a sturdier sort of vagabond who carries a stout cudgel as well as his wand. Of the Fool's attributes the one that interests me the most is the wallet that hangs from the wand over his shoulder. I myself am a great accumulator of bags and rucksacks of all kinds, I don't feel right unless I'm somewhat burdened. I'd even go so far as to say that a writer needs to be burdened – the writing is after all the unburdening. To my way of thinking our Fool may flaunt himself on the brink as much as he likes but eventually he must discard the rose, must leave the flower of his youth behind to wilt in the sunshine while he takes his burden and climbs laboriously down into the abyss to get to work. His number, after all, is Zero, a round nothingness which he must fill with the world of his perception.

The wallet is a magic one, he himself doesn't know what's in it but it's heavy with the past, present, and future of the universe; in it is a jumble of unformed words and images, of colours and sounds and strangeness, continually arranging itself in new combinations wanting to be worlds. His real journey begins when he opens the wallet and it swallows him up in its darkness where he must make his way through time and chance, must keep himself empty and knowing nothing so that in that magic darkness the universe can continually fill the Zero of him with itself. He must persist in his folly until, as William Blake said, he becomes wise. And that wisdom lies in knowing how and when to know nothing and be open to everything.

Sometimes the question arises: what's it all about, where are we going and is there any point to the whole thing? Thinking isn't much help, you have to fly by the seat of your pants, you have to feel it. To me it feels as if all of us inhabit and are inhabited by one universal mind, we are all receptors of a universal transmission. Some of us tune into more of it, some less, but it wants to be received, it wants to be perceived and we are its organ of perception. Surely we haven't yet received the whole transmission, surely we haven't tuned into all of its frequencies.

Here we are on a planet that was clean and beautiful and we've defiled it; we're killing the world-child, we're committing terricide. Perhaps this earth will last long enough for the first space colonies to be founded and send their probes further and further out into our galaxy and beyond. We planet-killers are the seekers and the finders and we've got to go on finding, inside and outside the self, what it's all about. We must go into the dark and magic wallet of time within which we shall find that bleak and dreadful room where the paper bear waits to gobble us up. We must go into all the scary places to find ourselves, we fools, we must encounter all that lives there, and if we never find our way out again it will still have been a risk worth taking, more than that: it's the risk we're born for, made for. It's the risk we owe it to ourselves to take. We've called up what we can't put down and now we've got to look into its eyes and talk to it.

It would be quite natural at this point if you rose up and demanded to know what this exhortation is about in pragmatic terms: what do I want from you? I want to encourage you, if you're not already doing it, to help enlarge the limited-reality consensus. I don't read much contemporary fiction so I'm not really qualified to have an opinion, but I believe that too much of it is simply the conveying of chunks of experience wrapped up in some kind of story. What the world needs more of, although my royalty statements indicate that it doesn't as yet recognise the need, is writing that tries to find out what's what by paying attention to the images that live under the picture-cards that we conventionally exchange and the images that appear beyond where we ordinarily look, the occulting glimmers under the reasonable thought and beyond the ordinary range of thought, the words that twist and moan and dance and sing behind the words that go out through our mouths, and the unknown words that we sometimes almost hear from far away, the mysteries that move us, and the patterns of the dance that lives us.

I'm encouraging you to have a go because I think – and I could well be wrong – that some writers are afraid to let themselves go that way. Years ago, when I sometimes did workshops, I found people who were quite good with words but they clung to safe structures, they remained unobsessed, they were not driven to write. To do the kind of writing that extends the recognised boundaries of reality you have to be obsessed, you have to let ungraspable ideas take you in their jaws and shake you around, you have to try all kinds of things, most of which don't work, to get them down on paper, and when you do get them down on paper you'll have to rewrite them fifteen or sixteen times because they won't be right the first time. And very likely you'll have to do something else to pay the rent. I could never have afforded to write novels if I hadn't built up an economic base with children's picture books; there simply aren't that many people who want to read the kind of thing I write, although there are more now than there used to be.

A writer sitting at a desk is nothing very heroic and yet you have to find ways of feeling heroic because the effort required certainly is. I want a heroic image to end this with, so out of the dust of mortality and the darkness of the magic wallet I bring a column of horsemen borrowed from the end of one of John Wayne's best films, *She Wore a Yellow Ribbon*, John Ford's wonderful elegy for the US cavalry (with screenplay by Frank Nugent and Laurence Stallings from the story by James Warner Bellah). Listen to the music, listen to the sound of their hooves and the slap and jingle of harness as the horsemen pass by and the voice-over narrator says:

So here they are, the dogfaced soldiers, the regulars, the fifty-cents-a-day professionals, riding the outposts of a nation from Fort Reno to Fort Apache, from Sheridan to Stark. They were all the same, men in dirty-shirt blue, and only a cold page in the history books to mark their passing. But wherever they rode and whatever they fought for, that place became the United States.

Well, here we are, Manitoba writers. The bugle is sounding boots and saddles, it always is. So climb on to your horses and be the kind of writing fools of whom it can be said: wherever they wrote and whatever they sought for, that place became the world.

1987

Word Pix

The Skeleton on the Tracks

This first picture is stolen from Max Klinger (1857–1920). Klinger did an etching-aquatint, *On the Tracks*, in which a skeleton lies nonchalantly across railroad tracks, sucking one finger and looking down the line towards where one might suppose a train to be approaching. Mountains in the distance; silence; maybe one or two sound effects of birds.

But this isn't the same as that: in this picture the naked skeleton is tied hand and foot and it's screaming, screaming, screaming. 'O my God!' it screams, 'O my God! If the train hits me I'll come alive!' Is the skeleton a man or a woman? One doesn't know yet, one isn't close enough for a good look.

This word-picture is an etching also. Think of it like that. No colours, just blacks and whites and greys, scratched on a metal plate with a needle. Eaten out with acid, the plate pressed as if sexually into the paper, the image imprinted, the skeleton's silent screaming echoing through the thick white paper.

Five Roads

There's a room that's empty except for five pictures on one wall. Not an inviting number, five – not magical like seven, not hermetic like four. Uncomfortably five. Five pictures.

Not paintings but etchings, drawn with a needle, eaten out with acid. Black and white and grey tones comprising fine scratchings.

Roads are what the pictures are of. Empty roads. Nothing on them. Roads through high and jagged mountains, roads across level plains. Winding roads and straight ones. You can walk into any of these pictures and you'll find yourself composed of etched lines, delicate greys, walking (or running if you choose and if you can) to wherever the road takes you. Perhaps you can enter by one picture and come out by another, I don't know.

Perhaps you never can come out once you enter the silence of those pictures.

The Sphinks

There's a huge black-and-white bird called a sphinks. That's the right spelling. Maybe it has a lion's head, I don't know. Or maybe it's a pterodactyl, I'm not sure. Anyhow, this great huge bird eats paper and drinks ink and it shits words.

Here's a solitary traveller crossing the etching of a grey desert maybe, under a dazzling white sun and he hears the horrid squawk of the sphinks high in the white and pitiless sky and he cowers and covers his head but it's no use. Splat! A direct hit: the word QUASI. In capitals. QUASI. All over him. What is he to do with that? It isn't even a mirage, it's real. QUASI. Not a camel in sight, not a Land Rover. Not a camera crew. Nothing. Can he be intrepid? Quasi-intrepid?

At This Point

At this point one tries to put something together. What the hell, one's only human. There's the skeleton on the tracks. Has it got long blonde hair, is it a seductive young blonde female skeleton in distress? Yes, one thinks it is. Oh, sexy blonde skeleton bound hand and foot across the tracks and screaming, screaming, 'Who will save me from certain life?' Does one hear the train coming, hear that lonesome whistle wailing down the desert wind and echoing in the mountains? One thinks one hears it.

Now one understands the room with the five pictures, the five roads. Does one of those roads lead to this screaming blonde skeleton? Or all of them? How much time is there before the train arrives and the skeleton's young death is over, finished, oh the pity of it? So young, so beautiful, so naked and with blonde hair streaming in the sound of that lonesome whistle down the desert wind and echoing in the mountains.

One has entered one of the pictures, the third from the left. That was how the solitary traveller (that's who one is) came to be shat upon by the sphinks. And now, covered in QUASI, this solitary traveller staggers on in the hope of performing, against all odds, a quasi-rescue. Incurable quasi-romantic.

The Sea, the Sea, the Wild and Stormy Sea

O my God, how did the sea come into it; one was just getting used to the roads and the quasi-shit and all that. O my God the sea – one wasn't prepared for it, it wasn't in any of the five pictures, there was no hint whatever that it was going to be part of the sequence. Big, surging, not to be denied, black and wild in the night under the black wind and no moon. One is so afraid on this what? Raft? Bit of wreckage? Lugger? What? One doesn't think one could handle a lugger and a raft seems, I don't know, uninteresting. So it's a bit of wreckage rising up, up, up on the huge waves then dropping down, down, down sickeningly in the trough. One hates this, one is even more afraid of the sea than of the empty wasteland through which the road was winding.

What now?

By a Tremendous Effort of the Will one Quells

By a tremendous effort of the will one quells the raging tempest, calms the stormy sea, forces it below the appearance of things until it surges into dunes and mountains, into wasteland over which the long road winds. But it's still there under the appearance of things, heaving the landscape and making one seasick.

Here at last is the railroad, receding across the bulging and heaving landscape to a vanishing point where undoubtedly the beautiful blonde skeleton lies screaming on the tracks. If only the sea will agree to stay under the appearance of things until one reaches the vanishing point and rescues the skeleton!

The Enormous Inevitable Here and Now

Now for the quasi-rescue that I, the solitary traveller, hope to effect. I can see how it's going to be: here comes the locomotive, filling the whole picture in one's eyes, the enormous inevitable here and now of it, the smoke and steam of it, the noise and the smell of it, the hard steel and rivets of it. EEEEEEEEEEEEEEEEEEE, the shriek of it dopplering towards her, towards me as I stand over her.

This has got to be perfectly timed. My Swiss-Army knife is in my hand, poised intrepidly to cut the ropes that tie her to the tracks. Now it's happening, happeninggggggggggghhhhhrr-RRRROWWWWHOOOSH! Yes! The bright blade slashes through her bonds, the locomotive strikes her, her death is immediately ended and she is alive and blonde and beautiful and smelling good, altogether a juicy armful in my arms as I leap with her on to the locomotive's cowcatcher. Only as an etching can I do this – in my ordinary fleshly state I'm too slow and heavy.

'Oh,' says my firm and bouncy ex-skeleton, wearing nothing but a startled expression. 'Life has hit me like a locomotive.'

'Yes,' I say, 'that's pretty much what happened.'

'I'm alive!' she says. 'And to think that I was afraid of this! How wonderful you are!'

'No exclamation points are necessary, madam,' I say. 'One has only done what any quasi-hero would have done.'

'But how can I ever thank you?'

'Please,' I say. 'People are reading this even as we speak.' With what velocity we rush off the page and into the unknown together, bands playing and flags of all nations flying on either side as the locomotive shrieks and shrieks its madness and its quasi-joy that now this seven-picture quasi-adventure is successfully concluded.

1991

Fragments of a Lament
for Thelonious Monk

Here I am sitting in front of my computer monitor looking at dates and times in luminous green letters on the screen. I've typed a memo of travel and engagements into the computer. From my tape recorder comes music with that bright OK sound that you hear from the curtained screen in the cinema before the lights are dimmed. It is, yes, it is also that music you hear in the echoing and vasty spaces of airports. It makes me feel good, makes me feel neither here nor there but comfortably in between. Airports have many monitors with arrival and departure times on their screens, flights designated by letters and numbers in luminous characters that don't move but are full of subliminal motion, full of dancingness and quivering.

Here at my desk I've put together that airport feeling, that wonderful airport state of mind, everything for the present suspended, the traveller out of reach of the usual daily bother, out of reach of all those daily systems by which the extraordinary is reduced to a grey and manageable tedium.

Not everything is suspended; no, only the grey and manageable tedium is suspended; the extraordinary is once more available to the soul that is hungry and thirsty for it. Yes, yes, anything at all may happen now. The hitherto unrecognised may suddenly be recognised. The ungraspable mountain may suddenly present itself to one's vision. Transcendence!

Listening now to an effigy of Thelonious Monk, a dome of the dummy world, that midnight dome, those caves of nice. Always the slant rhyme with Thelonious, that was his Thelonious assault on the grey and civil devils of the ordinary. Walk tall and slanty, Thelonious; you live.

There was a little bit of spring sunshine, and already the girls were on their summer legs, the ravishing Persephones of the Fulham Road on their beckoning and procreative summer legs, trundling their goodies in the thin, in the vernal, in the London sunshine, and I went into what looked like a record shop. I shaped words with my lips in the noise to the smiling and undoubtedly deaf young man, I don't remember what words were on his T-shirt at first. WE HAVE NO THELONIOUS MONK maybe, I don't know. I shaped the words, 'Have you got any Thelonious Monk?'

Shake of his head, smiling, uncaring, deaf.

'Call yourself a record shop and you haven't got any Thelonious Monk?'

THERE IS NO SUCH THING AS THELONIOUS MONK, said his T-shirt.

Thelonious Monk! Ah! Thelonious! How you are gone, how I lament your death now! You are of the fabric of my perception, yes that is not too much to say. In The Five Spot in Cooper Square I sat long ago in the blue smoke and the buzz of night-murmurers and saw you under your magical hat at the helm, your keyboard was the wheel by which you steered precariously our frail vessel on the edgelines of the actual. Peerless navigator, ardent darer that you were, dark albatross of the farther frequencies.

The letters on the screen of my computer are made up of a continual dancing; letter by letter I see my thoughts appear on the screen. My thoughts and the mind that thinks them are equally composed of the dancing; the dancing is there before anything else. You are in that dancing, Thelonious

Monk, in that green dancing in which letter by letter my thoughts appear this midnight, round about this midnight mindnight. On the margin of the moment where you made notations, Thelonious, at The Five Spot in Cooper Square in the rain and in the fog when I was young.

1983

Portknockie

Like the fungal hyphae that anchor lichens to rock there are ideas all dense and intertwined that grip us to the rock of existence; one of them is the idea of return, the idea that something once seen can be returned to significantly. What was seen, what might be the significance? We don't know, we are uncertain, we want to go back for another look.

In 1967 I saw Portknockie; in 1979 I wanted to see it again. All places begin with a night journey; I booked a sleeping compartment on the *Aberdonian* departing King's Cross 22.15, arriving in Dundee 09.15. Having been invited by a university I was going to Dundee to talk; having been invited by silence and the remembered wind I was going to Portknockie to listen.

Portknockie, with its idea of return beating in it like a heart, is itself an idea that beats like a heart in the larger body of things: it is the idea of living on the sea, by the sea, for the sea, and with the sea; it is the idea of getting a living and a dying from the sea, of continuing seaward and seawise regardless. A rocky shore of red cliffs, green humps and hillocks, shags and gulls above the green and marbling water foaming in among the names and bulks of landmarks: Green Castle, Port Hill, Bow Fiddle, rising from the sea. Dark and urgent the shags fly with long necks extended. The dark wings on the downstroke make an upside-down V; on the upstroke a right-side-up V; the downstroke and the upstroke make a dark X through which the body of the bird shoots like an arrow. The gulls descant above the foam and spray, their voices topographical, like contour lines in the air. The luggers are gone, the herring are gone.

The idea of Portknockie ascends from the simple geometry and arithmetic of its harbour, a tested formula that is like a spell, like words of stone and concrete to shelter boats from the sea: the breakwaters of the outer harbour and the inner harbour; the outflung arm of another breakwater beyond the outer harbour; the gaps where the boats pass from the wildness to the calm.

The houses of Portknockie rank themselves with thrifty slates above the harbour, like a congregation whose altar is below them. The top floor of the Hythe Hotel affords a view of the sea with chimney-pots and starlings in the foreground. The window of the hotel room and the hotel itself are not known to me as I think about Portknockie in the sleeping-car, as I think about Portknockie in my little onward cabin of night. By day the towns we pass will be distinct and individual; by day the towns and places may or may not be of the present moment; but by night, dark trees against the sky or clustered lights they are all one thing, they are of the night and in the night belong at once to memory.

Having talked in Dundee I went to listen in Portknockie. I hired a car and headed north. At Montrose I turned north-west into the Grampians and the Cairn o' Mount road. Early May this was, wood-sorrel and primrose in the woods to the south. Over the mountains hung a blue-grey rain curtain against which soared white gulls. The rain once entered became sleet and snow. Winter abated and revealed a cruising owl low above the heather. People talk lightly of owls, poets have them for their stock-in-trade but other than in zoos I've only seen three owls in my life and this was the third: a tawny owl with a proper flat owl face on the front of it like a scanner in the clear grey air over the heather and the sedge at half past four in the afternoon. Coming out of the mountains I see, far from any strand, an oyster-catcher sitting on a post. The car passes within a few feet of it but it doesn't move until I turn and come back for another look, then it flies slowly away. And all of this is on the way to Portknockie, Portknockie hasn't happened yet.

When I come out of the mountains I feel an easing of tension; my relief shows me how much stronger than I knew was my craving for the open and the sea.

Then there is Portknockie and the top-floor hotel window with its view of chimney-pots, starlings, and sea: unknown in the sleeping-car but known now. Now with two large gins in me I roll pleasantly down Victoria Street towards the headland called the Green Castle. Knowing as I go that the idea of return may be wholly an illusion, that return may not be possible at all. Knowing that place itself may not be possible at all, that all the place there is may well be no more than the moving point of consciousness in us, that looking in its cage of bone that looks out through our eye-holes.

Then there is the sea, the green and marbling, the foaming and the milky water beating on the rocks and clattering the beach stones in its backward suck, the stones that click and clatter under my feet. Bones there are too, sea-bones rounded by the grinding tidewash and the stones: bones of what? Sheep, cattle, dogs? I don't know. But place is possible, and return; even a moon, a little misty moon. I find myself saying, 'Ah! Ah! Ah! I'm so glad!'

Why such gladness? I don't know why Portknockie should have any special significance for me. When I was there twelve years ago I was writing copy for a scotch whisky; my companions were an art director and a photographer. I climbed the Green Castle; I was shown brown photographs by an old fisherman; I was not aware that anything in particular had happened. The place stayed in my mind and pulled me back to it. What is this idea of return? To what am I returning that I should exclaim with gladness? I don't know, I can't

say. How does it feel then? 'It is a movement and a rest.'
Those words describe it accurately; they are from Logion 50
of the Coptic *Gospel of Thomas* found at Nag Hammadi in
Upper Egypt in 1945:

> Jesus said: If they say to you: Whence have you come?,
> tell them: We have come from the light, the place where
> the light came into being through itself alone. It [stood],
> and it revealed itself in their image. If they say to you:
> Who are you?, say: We are his sons, and we are the elect
> of the living Father. If they ask you: What is the sign of
> your Father in you?, tell them: It is a movement and a
> rest.*

The last line of Logion 50 is for me the very essence
of return; not so the lines leading up to it: the sea, the
strand, the shapen rocks and headlands are not, for me, of
the Father and the light but of darkness and the Mother —
the Old Mother, Great Mother, Mother Goddess, womb of
everything and nurturing body of earth.

Still, why the gladness? Returning to the womb of sea and
darkness would be death and not yet welcome to me; this
gladness is a lively feeling. I think it may be that emanations
of origin make us glad, that we are glad to recognise in movement and in rest the womb of all motion, the genetrix of that
potential energy from which the spark jumps at conception
to begin the last stage of the night journey that brings us to
the place of birth.

Just as the dome of St Paul's Cathedral has its Whispering
Gallery that transmits sound, just as wet weather holds and
intensifies smells, so the topography of Portknockie's shapen
humps and stony hollows, the rise and fall of its ground,
holds, intensifies, and transmits the emanations of its origin

---

New Testament Apocrypha, Volume One, edited by E. Hennecke
and W. Schneemelcher. English Translation edited by R. McL. Wilson,
SCM Press Ltd, 1963.

and our own. In doing this it provides a cross-over between the seen and the unseen, between the potential and the kinetic energies of that space we move in which is not simply space: perhaps it is the soul of the universe; and we are the organ of perception required by that soul.

The fancy offers itself that Portknockie has taken on this power only since declining from its worldly success. Perhaps when it was a thriving herring port this power was not in it; it had first to lose the specialised power of what we recognise as useful function before it could manifest the power of the potential, the power of the one continuous rhythm of immanent change and permutation that vibrates behind the appearances of things. Indifferent to us it is, inhuman; yet to tune ourselves to it feels good, gives us a sense of release from the hard bargain of the mortal contract. Perceiving then the full nature of the power I abandon the fancy of its accession; I know that this power of the potential has always been in Portknockie. It was here when the nets were heavy with fish and the brown sails prospered, but at that time when the harbour was forested with the masts of Zulu boats and resounded with strong shouts it would have been less apparent. Now the silent empty harbour shows itself to us and requires our attention.

All round Portknockie harbour are great iron rings secured by iron eyes to concrete and to stone, iron rings nearly as thick as my wrist and with an aperture more than a foot across. Here I look at one of them much older than the others, it lies flat on the concrete by the inner harbour wall, thick flakes of brown rust on it like tree-bark, the outer roundness of it rusted into flatnesses and angles like a rough thick vine or a branch bent in a circle. The iron eye that holds the ring is also like old wood, like a branch thrust up through the concrete and doubling back into it. What does it say, this iron-into-wood? It says what the ribs and columns of the crypt of Canterbury Cathedral say: those stone columns are the trunks, those stone ribs of the vaulting are the branches,

they are the living wood of Christ and year-king become trees
of stone. They say what this iron-become-wood says: Now I
show it to you this way, now I show it to you that way.

1981

Footplacers, London Transport
Owls, Wincer-Boise

Why do some people take care not to step on the cracks in the paving while others take no notice whatever of the cracks? One says 'cracks' but of course they are not cracks; they are the edges where, apparently, one square of paving ends and another begins. That one calls them cracks is significant; it betokens a recognition of a surface that might be broken through, a surface that keeps separate the overness from an underness in which move creatures of the other in ways not to be understood by us. Who has not at one time or another sensed in that dark otherness, sometimes quaint and solemn, sometimes mad and strangely echoing, the footplacer? Yes, yes, the footplacer: in the concrete underfoot it lives and walks, not in hollow spaces but molecularly in the solid concrete; particularly it is to be found in the concrete station-platforms of the underground; it is upside-down to us and we are upside-down to it as it places its feet softly one by one against our pacing feet. Perhaps it thinks of us as being the reflection or the shadow of its own walking; perhaps footplacers talking amongst themselves call *us* footplacers, think of us as strange beings who walk upside-down aboveground softly placing our feet one by one against theirs. The footplacer is a cumulative creature; as it places its feet against our feet all the footsteps of our lives are added up and gathered into it. Where did we go and when? What did we do there? All those footsteps have been gathered up into the footplacer, all those goings that are gone.

So much walking there is in a great city, so many footsteps! Sometimes from the escalators in the underground there comes a cry like the hooting of an owl, and indeed it is an owl that cries but not a small and feathered one: the owls that one hears in the escalators are the treadmill owls; they are made of steel and nickel, brass and copper; they weigh a ton or more; they are at least eight feet tall and they smell of machine oil. Great dark glistening things they are, all gleaming joints and pistons – one can't imagine them hatching from an egg. No one knows where they came from; it is believed that they were there in the subterranean dark long before the underground was built. When the tunnels were opened they came blinking into the light, indicating by gestures that they were peaceful and wanted to work. They were accordingly set to walking great treadmills that powered the endlessly ascending and descending stairs, and there they have remained ever since, walking their treadmills. No one knows whether they are living creatures or intelligent machines; no one knows how long they live or how long they last. No one knows what they do when the underground is closed. No one knows whether or not they can fly. No one knows if anyone has ever seen them.

Wincer-boise also are creatures of the underground but there is nothing dark about them, nothing heavy. Wincer-boise is a collective name; there are many of them. They are called boise because there is something boyish about them and they make a noise; possibly they *are* a noise, one can't say for certain because they cannot be seen. London Transport does not acknowledge their presence, and whatever their function may be it is entirely unofficial. They live among the rails of the underground and they become greatly excited at the approach of a train; it is then that their strange wincing cry is heard:

'Wheats-yew, wheats-yew!' They spring up onto the rails and race ahead of the train, only turning aside into the tunnel niches just before the next station so that the wincer-boise waiting there can have their sport in turn. Wincer-boise seem to be especially active on dry cold days.

Here we have not the space in which to take up the matter of those variously shaped and patterned iron plates in the pavement, some of which tilt up a little under the pressure of a footstep and fall back with that characteristic sound well known by those who lie awake in the small hours of the night. On some of these plates there appear the raised iron letters LEB or NTGB; some spell out whole words such as POST OFFICE TELEPHONES. When LEB means LONDON ELECTRICITY BOARD and when it means LET ENTROPY BE, when NTGB means NORTH THAMES GAS BOARD and when it means NOTHING TO GO BACK – such aspects of the traffic between the underness and the overness of London cannot be dealt with here.

1982

Mnemosyne, Teen Taals, and Tottenham Court Road

All India Radio broadcasts to Europe and the United Kingdom daily from 1745 to 2230 GMT on a frequency of 11,620 kHz. I listen to it almost every day and I record as much music as I can. Sometimes reception is beautifully clear, and the chromatic splendours of the classical Karnatak style build palaces of sound all round me in my Fulham workroom. Swaying painted elephants and iridescent peacocks, chanting priests, multitudes of worshippers, solitary mystics and astronomers, saffron-veiled beauties and dancers with ankle bells glisten in the misty drizzle of the London night outside my window, all India vivid with my ignorance. Great wild eastern dawns and screaming birds rise where the red and green lights of the District Line wink to the passing of the golden windows rumbling townwards, rumbling homewards. Distant passengers, perhaps seen every day, perhaps never to be seen again, pass in the passing windows among the painted elephants and the clash of ankle bells, the marble and the filigrees. At other times the ionosphere is unfavouring: Shiva as Destroyer, Kali with her necklace of skulls, garish polychrome demons dance in my short-wave receiver, roaring and crackling and filling the room with chaos which is, after all, to be expected; I accept it without complaint.

On the night of January 18th on 11,620 kHz there came across the more than four thousand miles of night air between Delhi and London in the General Overseas Service of All India Radio an illustrated talk devised, written, and presented by V. Petanjali: *The Concept of Time in Indian Music*. Having been pondering that very matter for the last year or so I wanted to hear what Mr Petanjali had to say but I was able to hear only a little; most of his talk was lost in the crackle and roar of the deities and demons of the air. Of the intelligible remainder much disappeared into the abyss between a dinner guest and my remembering to put a fresh tape cassette into the recorder. Some of his words, however, were not lost: while my wife and I and our friend ate sweet-and-sour spare ribs and drank red wine my Yaesu FRG-7000 communications receiver listened to Delhi and my Uher CR240 listened to the FRG-7000. The next morning when I played back the tape I had Mr Petanjali's opening words. Here they are:

> To talk about the time concept in Indian music I have to begin at the very beginning: in the rotation of planets, in the cycle of time, in the very cosmic design the ancient Indians discerned a fascinating rhythmic pattern. They felt proud about their knowledge, and in great reverence placed a drum, called *damaru*, in the hands of Lord Shiva, a god of their trinity.

There followed music and the beginning of Mr Petanjali's detailed exposition, which was soon lost in the roar and the crackle. I contented myself with Shiva's drum; that alone was enough for me; the idea of it, conveyed from a four thousand miles-distant mind by radio waves reflected from the ionosphere, immediately began to exist everywhere in my mind, my mind that recognises its own action as emanating from the beat of that cosmic drum.

Heinrich Zimmer in his book *Myths and Symbols in Indian Art and Civilization* describes South Indian bronzes of Shiva-Nataraja dating from the tenth and twelfth centuries AD.

This is Shiva as Lord of the Dance, gesturing conventionally with his double arms as he dances in a ring of flame upon the prostrate body of a dwarfish demon:

> The upper right hand, it will be observed, carries a little drum, shaped like an hour-glass, for the beating of the rhythm. This connotes Sound, the vehicle of speech, the conveyor of revelation, tradition, incantation, magic and divine truth. Furthermore, Sound is associated in India with Ether, the first of the five elements. Ether is the primary and most subtly pervasive manifestation of the divine Substance. Out of it unfold, in the evolution of the universe, all the other elements, Air, Fire, Water, and Earth. Together, therefore, Sound and Ether signify the first, the truth-pregnant moment of creation, the productive energy of the Absolute, in its pristine, cosmogenetic strength.

Shiva's drum beats time and creates sound which is the vehicle of speech and the conveyor of revelation, tradition, incantation, magic, and divine truth – all of which rely on or collaborate with memory. With the gyroscope of memory we navigate our forward course both mental and physical, whether from bathroom to kitchen, Tchaikovsky to Bach, or ten leagues beyond the wide world's end. Through memory we refer, we connect, we recall, we retain, we bring back, we hold on to. Mnemosyne is Memory and she is the mother of the nine muses because all of our arts and sciences – all of what we are and where we are – comes from the womb of memory spiralled in the double helix of human genetics and the collective conscious and unconscious experience of the human race.

The etymology of such a word as *memory* is bound to be worth looking into; there will always be surprises. *Memory* comes, by way of Middle French, from the Latin *memoria* – *memor* meaning mindful. It is akin to the Old English *gemimor* meaning well-known; *mimorian* to remember; the

Middle Dutch *mimeren* to muse, brood; the Latin *mora* delay; the old Irish *airmert* prohibition; the Greek *mermēra* trouble; and the Sanskrit *smarati* he remembers.

Delay, prohibition, trouble! *Mora, airmert, mermēra*! Yes, indeed – how often memory delays and is delayed, prohibits and is prohibited, troubles and makes trouble!

And returning to Heinrich Zimmer and Shiva-Natarāja, what do we find in his description of the prostrate dwarfish demon on whom Shiva dances? Zimmer says:

> This is Apasmāra Purusha, 'The Man or Demon (*purusa*) called Forgetfulness or Heedlessness (*apasmāra*)'. It is symbolical of life's blindness, man's ignorance. Conquest of this demon lies in the attainment of true wisdom. Therein is release from the bondages of the world.

So Shiva's prostrate demon, the demon that must be conquered, is forgetfulness. And yet we remember, we do not forget, that the word *memory* in its rolling ramble on the roads of speech and time has picked up and gathered to itself *mora, airmert*, and *mermēra*: delay, prohibition, trouble.

Memory is the natural and necessary partner of music. Music is a puissant recaller of time past; music is memory's sister and for its very life relies on memory to hold in our minds the passage of sounds through time.

Shiva's drum beats time, makes sound for music to live in, music that lives by memory, or at least in our usage it *seems* to live by memory. Certainly when we listen back inside our heads for Mario Cavaradossi pacing the battlements of the Castel Sant'Angelo and singing '*E lucevan le stelle*', we are invoking memory, or when we listen back for a Chopin mazurka or even a Bach cantata. When we come to such as Bach's *The Art of Fugue*, however, something else enters into it: we find ourselves not so much retracing a track of note-by-note sound as experiencing a mode of being to which sound is a rite of passage and a way of the spirit to a place beyond music, a place where memory cannot reach, where every time is now. The music that puts us in that place does not depend on memory; it is without greed, makes no demands; it doesn't ask to be remembered. By such music Apasmāra Purusha – who is Forgetfulness and Heedlessness, who is life's blindness and man's ignorance – is overwhelmed, defeated, crushed beneath our foot at the very outset because there is no need to remember, nothing to remember: there is only being and the flicker of time/no time, dance and stillness.

An exemplary form of the ungreedy, not-asking-to-be-remembered kind of music is the Indian time cycle: the *teen taal*, the *jhap taal*, and other rhythmic patterns. Keep in mind that this is not a scholar's analysis: I am not a scholar nor am I taking in the music in a scholarly way. It comes to me varying in the strength and clarity of its signal according to sun-spots, weather, and interference; its transmission and reception seem a paradigm of the heart's desire in a dark wood full of dangers. Wounded, broken, near dismembered, it arrives sometimes, and always I await it with a lover's hopes and fears. I listen to All India Radio addictively and indiscriminately: ragas; folk songs; song hits from the silver screen; news; commentary; talks on drought, famine, and holy days – anything, even cricket test match resumés. I do it because that music has made all of All India Radio interesting to me. I never know in what form it will turn up, that music that takes me to the place deeper than memory. Most often it's the time cycles but often it happens in the vocal and instrumental ragas and sometimes in folk songs, particularly those of Manipur.

What's happened is that I've come to a time when I don't want much emotion in my music; I don't require either to be uplifted or downput by it. I find myself not listening to my favourite Bach, Haydn, Mozart, Beethoven, Schubert, Chopin. I don't want much emotion; I want the dance in the stone. That's how I think of it: the dance in the stone; not the foam forever fading in the wake of our forward motion. As I write this I'm listening to Haydn's String Quartet Opus 54 No. 2 in C; it is lean, muscular, brilliantly brooding; the adagio always breaks my heart. But I find that breaking the heart with music isn't the thrill it once was. What I'm after more and more is on the other side of heartbreak; it's in the stone of things, with bare, spare music that not only doesn't ask to be remembered, it doesn't ask for anything at all, makes no attempt to hold on to the hearer or anything else. It moves to the beat of Shiva's drum, which is after all nothing especially eastern or exotic; it is only that same everyday drum in the heart of the atom, the same in Hammersmith as in Hyderabad, moving to the beat of the stillness in the dance and the dance in the stillness.

Of the Indian time cycles the sparest and barest are those performed on the *tabla*, the two drums often heard in accompaniment of the sitar. In the *teen taal* I most admire, the drums, played by Alla Rakha, are the foreground instruments, providing a constantly varying percussion against the unvarying melodic continuo of unknown wind instruments. The continually varying sameness of the *teen taal* gives us the alternating of stillness and dance that is the audible flicker of what we call time. Hearing this music I remember having molecules and atoms explained for the first time, how the wooden table that looks and feels so solid, so much the very essence of tangible everyday reality, is in fact a phantom table, a table of illusion, the very sketchiest transparency of the ghost of a table in which molecules and atoms glance and ricochet, whizzing silently in the figures of the table dance. I remember my astonishment at leaning my elbows on the table dance, on the transparent ghost of the thing, on the whizzing lightning interplay of particles that agree, by courtesy only and as a favour, to dance in the shape of a table for a while. I remember amazement at the spilling of milk and the spooning up of porridge on that metaphysical accommodation in the shape of a table. All of that is in the flicker of the stillness and the dance that is the *teen taal* that doesn't ask to be remembered, doesn't try to hold on, offers its steady flicker without greed and without assumption.

The Indian time cycle offers a continually unassuming repetition with its modest but seemingly infinite variation and permutation. This continual repetition sets all clocks at nought, defeats all haste and hurry, gives us a place to be. We are not remorselessly and implacably hurried along on a track of mortal tragedy. Because that is after all the mortal tragedy, that the foam is continually fading in the wake, that the moment will not stay.

The moment will not stay. We seek out places where the sorrow will be lessened, places where there is heart's ease in the sorrow, heart's comfort amidst the pain. For good or ill the moment will not stay. How fast the world flees in all directions from us! How can we hold on to just a little more world, only a little. It isn't much to ask.

With hardware, with machines, with steel precision, with nickel-cadmium, with digital readouts and light-emitting diodes we hope to grip the slippery sea-goddess moment that slides so smoothly through our longing, through our lusting and our lonesome fingers. There are places to which we go for what we need: there is Tottenham Court Road.

Along Tottenham Court Road drift men with hungry faces, hungry eyes, and I among them. Drifting, pausing, looking, hoping, lusting for heart's ease, soul's comfort, all that gleams and flaunts its steely-satin lustre in the shining windows of the shops in Tottenham Court Road. Tottenham Court Road! Street of sin, street of shame! I go there by underground, rumbling beneath the surface, howling through black tunnels. I emerge into the light of those windows of desire gleaming in the winter dusk. Heart's ease! Soul's comfort! Precision, weight, accuracy, professional quality! There is so much I need, so much I want, and all of it is here in my street of love and lust, of audio and video, of high fidelity, of liquid crystal display and digital readout.

How shall I speak my heart? I want so much, need so much!

I need circuitry and calibration and oscillations of quartz: I need synthesisers and equalisers; I need whatever is the very latest development, because whatever I have is not quite the very latest development, not quite the state-of-the-art thing, not truly the reference model.

I need a quartz digital watch with a liquid crystal display in a steel case weighing five pounds, bound together with quarter-inch thick steel rivets and secured to my wrist with half-inch thick steel links. It must have a stop-watch function, a lap timer, and an alarm function. It must of course tell the day and the month and the time in principal cities all over the world. It must withstand pressures of five thousand pounds to the inch, must operate underwater to a depth of a mile and a half, and be perfectly resistant to the suckers of giant squids. It must not lose more than a tenth of a second per year. The watch I have now is useless: it loses three tenths of a second per year and it won't tell me the time in Kuala Lumpur.

I need, I need, I am faint with need and with desire. The calculator I have now won't do anything but add, subtract, multiply, and divide. I need one with a digital clock on it, and of course the clock must have the alarm function and the principal-cities capability. I need a square-root and a round-root function. I need both logarithms and plankarithms. I need in my calculator a memory that will retain not only the square roots, the round roots, the logarithms, and the plankarithms but also my passport number, mortgage number, life assurance number, car insurance number, car registration number, driver number, AA membership number, credit card numbers, current account number, cheque-card number, National Health Service number, telephone number, name, and address. Also it must tell me when and where the sales meeting is and who is selling what to whom. This calculator must be as thin as one side of a very thin sheet of paper or I can't use it. If it weighs more than a postage stamp it's no good to me.

Very thick watches and very thin calculators are what I need.

High fidelity. Never have I had fidelity of sufficient height, and I crave it. I require the fidelity of hundreds, of many, many symphony orchestras, all of them faithful from twenty to twenty thousand hertz and with watts enough to do it to my neighbour louder than he can do it to me. I need speakers as big as vans. What I'm after is that the reproduced sound be more original than the original. The original came and went like everything else; it was no more than a fleeting murmur in a doubting ear. I need professional quality pre-amplifiers and amplifiers and graphic equalisers; I need massive woofers and ultrasonic tweeters because I want nothing less than a sound that will extend rearward in time to replace the sound of which it is a recording, so that nothing whatever is lost. What's the use of holding back any longer? I want to duplicate the world. I want to have in reserve a second world that does not pass away. I want in sound and image the equivalent of that map that Jorge Luis Borges tells of, that map that was the same size as the country it was a map of.

Now you know, and I needn't go into all the rest of it; I needn't tell of the short-wave receiver that will pick up broadcasts from the South Pole or indeed from Jupiter if Jupiter is broadcasting. I needn't tell of the tape recorder that will listen to and record the receiver that will listen to Jupiter. I needn't tell of the filters and the antenna tuners and the trembling blue-lit needles of signal-strength meters and the tiny red and green and yellow glow of light-emitting diodes cosy in the night. I needn't tell of the teleprinter that plugs into the short-wave receiver and prints out the news on paper as it comes in. There's retention for you; there's world and passing moment held if you like. Ah! So much else I needn't tell of – the video-recorders and the cameras, the 800mm telephoto lenses and the infra-red capability for seeing in the dark and recording what is seen in the dark –

the owl's hunting and the mouse's death recorded with the price of gold, the fall of nations.

I've told you now and I feel better for the telling of it, so much better. There it is: one may control the habit but one doesn't change. I know what I am; I keep within decent limits – no more than one new major piece of equipment every six months and no more than three of the same thing, but I know I shall always be an equipment freak. I offer myself and my aberration for study so that others may come to understand this affliction that consumes me.

It isn't quite so bad as it was; if I live long enough I may possibly change. There may be other, more developed states of being. Possibly the only keeping is a constant letting go.

Possibly the only keeping is a constant letting go. If I speak now the name of something, how much will be in it for the hearer? If I say: the black-and-white bull of Evangelistrias. As I hear the words there seems to be world in them. Mule bells on the wind through the olive trees. The calling of the hooded crows and the sight of the sea through a notch in the mountains. World of the seen, world of the unseen.

The monastery chapel faced east. West of the altar down a steep and stony path was a spring of clear, cold mountain water like some paradigm of virtue. A crucifix in red was painted on the blue-shadowed rock; there were Greek words on a white stone tablet let into the rock from which the shining water gurgled sparkling over brown leaves, singing through its stone trough in the shade.

West of the altar was the spring. North was the sea, seen misty blue through the wooded mountains forested in recessive tones of green from the warmer foreground to the cooler distance. The most distant slope was the sparsest, the barest, the bluest before the sea. The sea seen from a mountain through a notch in mountains under the calling of hooded crows and the sighing of the wind is more world than can be taken in; one can only offer oneself to it.

East of the altar was the stable. Tethered near it were a young brown-and-white she-goat and a black mule with a tinkling bell. Some cows grazed nearby. Inside the stable in the breathy darkness was a black-and-white bull. He was lying on the straw with his back to me but when he became aware of me looking in through the window he scrambled to his feet, blowing out his warm breath, and turned to face me. He was chained to a stake with a chain that went round his horns. That black-and-white bull in the breathy darkness with a chain round his horns, that bull east of the altar in his stable on the shoulder of the mountain, that bull to be reached only by the steep ascent of a winding road, that bull seemed strong in significance, powerful in his references.

That monastery bull was the heart of the place for me and he became at once a place of the heart for me. His person became the heart of the place by virtue of his personal power and his ritual aspect. His mountain, his monastery, and his stable were on the island of Skiathos, a place between whose heart and mine nothing had happened up to that time. The bull was an epiphany that changed that. I felt privileged, awed, respectful.

I knew at once that the bull thus manifesting himself – horns and chain, breath and bollocks and pizzle in the breathy darkness – had entered me, had taken up a being at my centre, offering there his salutary magic and his unimpeachable power. I knew that nothing could be added to him or taken from him.

I must back up now and approach the bull again by way of the monastery. The Monastery of Evangelistrias on its mountain shoulder at the end of a rough and winding ascent is a manifestation of power. Whether you pray to other gods or to no gods you know it when you see it: the white walls and the cypresses, the pantiles and the slated roofs like tumuli – like breasts – the buildings of the complex holding themselves in steady converse with stone and tree and sky.

It was at the Monastery of Evangelistrias that the Greek flag was first flown in 1807, and it was with that flag that the oath was made to liberate Greece from Turkish domination. That mountain shoulder has the air of a stronghold that has defended itself; it has the look of a place that has paid its dues. The monastery has the presence of what people worship. It makes its claim upon the most casual visitor; it is serious, not to be trifled with. It makes unfaith and disbelief seem silly.

My attainment of the monastery/bull place of the heart was in three stages. On the first day that I saw Evangelistrias my family and I had driven up that rough and dusty road to find the monastery locked up. Its place was there, its place on which to stand; its spring was there, cold and clear; its bull was there, dark and patient; the monastery itself was closed. We tried the locked doors east and west, knocked, and got no answer. We walked all round it; we looked up at a dovecote rising from a ruined annexe. We admired the cypresses and the olive trees; we drank from the spring. Having only two exposures left in the camera I photographed an olive tree before finding the stable and the bull. That was the first stage.

The next day I came back alone with the camera, two rolls of film, and a tape recorder; I am after all, both by instinct and profession, a hunting-gathering animal. The equipment was modest; the camera was one I'd just given my wife for her birthday. It is not a professional instrument; she prefers something undemanding and simple to use. For the last ten years I have avoided buying myself a proper camera; I haven't wanted to over-excite myself. The tape recorder was the little cassette machine I use for a notebook.

Using my forty-eight exposures carefully I covered the subject reasonably well. First I photographed the approach on the brown road that wound through olive trees with glimpses of the tiled and slated roofs of Evangelistrias behind the cypresses. Having arrived I photographed the front and the entrance, then went through the now unlocked door into the courtyard with its carefully placed trees growing out of square apertures in the flagstones, their trunks white-washed to wainscot height. The trees grew up out of the stones and the stones rose up among the trees in compact stairs and arches, in white walls with dishes ornamentally let into them and slanting roofs of tile or breast-shaped slated roofs.

In one of the white walls of the courtyard was a shallow arched alcove in which there was a small arched niche painted red. In the niche was a tile with a Madonna and Child pictured in blue and white; the tile's white margin made it look like a large postage stamp. Just below the tile was a large square marble inlay which enclosed, with a black and white and red circular border, a black Greek cross with red rays on a white ground. The effect was like a compass rose. White arabesques on black filled out the corners of the square. Out of the centre of the black cross grew an iron water tap. There was a brown-painted cement trough under the tap, green plants on either side of it – one in a red pot and one in a large red tin can; a yellow melon by the red tin can. In front of the trough a yellow-handled mop stood in an olive-coloured plastic bucket as if confessing to the iron tap. Little trees on either side, not orange trees, arched towards each other in front of the arched alcove. There was a grape arbour as well, and as I backed up to photograph the red-painted niche I took into my field of view a low-hanging tendril of the vine swaying its green leaves in front of the face of the Virgin on the blue-and-white tile.

Seeing is not a simple thing, neither present sight nor sight recalled. I have been looking at my photographs as I write this: at the same time they give me what I didn't see and they take away what I did see. They take away the seeing of it; they present me with facts I cannot arrive at. Even if I put all fifty of them up on the wall in two rows of twenty-five or in five rows of ten or ten rows of five, I cannot take in all of them at once: moving my eyes from one to the next I lose the image as I go. If they lie in a stack on my desk, only the one on top is visible. If I have slides made, they'll be in a box waiting to be shown; if they're shown, they'll have only their brief moment of illumination. Why did I take the photographs? I wanted a world in reserve, nothing lost, everything stored for retrieval. I photographed all the buildings in the monastery compound so that I have the visual equivalent of a walk round the inside of the place. I photographed the chapel, its ikons, its candelabra, the vaulting of the ceiling. I went outside again and photographed the ruined annexe and the dovecote. I photographed the top of the mountain where the hooded crows were calling. I photographed the notch in the mountains and the misty blue where the sea was.

I thought: should I photograph the bull or shouldn't I? The bull was already both himself and the image of himself, I knew that. There was already in me a total recognition of that bull east of the altar, a total reception of his significance. It had already occurred to me that there is such a thing as conservation of significance. I knew, as I have written earlier, that nothing could be added to him or taken away from him. And yet . . . and yet I thought: why not be dead sure? (As I write this the thought comes to me that Othello will strangle Desdemona every time because he has simply got to have a dead certainty.) The lens and film I had were not fast enough to get a picture of the bull with the light available in the stable. I thought: shall I use flash? How can I possibly intrude on the privacy of that bull with flash? And if I do, what shall I get? It can only be a blank and wondering bull, diminished and robbed of his strong darkness by a silly flash of light.

I photographed the bull once without flash; that's why I don't actually have fifty prints from the fifty monastery exposures, only forty-nine. Then I photographed the bull once with flash. I have the print before me now as I write. There is the bull rendered flat on a piece of paper three and a half by five and an eighth inches, a tiny blank and wondering bull, diminished and robbed of his strong darkness by a silly flash of light. The causing of that diminished image of the bull to be stored on film for development later into tiny flatness constituted the second stage of my attainment of the monastery/bull place of the heart. Having done that I stood in front of the monastery looking towards the notch in the mountains and speaking my thoughts into the tape recorder.

I told myself that I'd done the bull no harm by photographing him; I hadn't taken anything away from him; if significance truly is conserved then I had lessened neither his nor mine. Yet I did something wrong, I know that. I interfered with something that doesn't want to be interfered with. That's the third stage: my knowing that my action with the monastery/bull place of the heart was incorrect.

Is it really necessary to bother this much about that place, that bull, and whether or not I acted correctly? I think it is. I think that all our capabilities were meant to be used, and I think that we are still evolving through the evolving use of our capabilities. We are the hunting and seeking animal; we are the sorting and pondering animal; we are the perceiver of the perceptible and the pursuer of the imperceptible, and our perceptions change us. It is in us to be continually more fine-tuned than we are, and the fine-tuning wants to happen.

I said that I had interfered with something that doesn't want to be interfered with. I sense that what I interfered with was the moving on of being; not the moving on of the being of the mountain or the monastery or the bull. No: it was the moving on of my own being that I interfered with when I tried to stop and hold and keep the present moment.

Just now while writing this I've misplaced my Evangelistrias photographs somewhere in the clutter on my desk; there's a flash of fear as my fingers scrabble for them. Once you've tried to stop and record the speeding moment with machines then you're lumbered with things that can be lost: bits of celluloid and paper; reels of tape. Once they're lost you feel as if you've lost some of the substance of those moments. And indeed you have lost it – you've lost it in the very act of trying to keep it. Oh, there's something dreadfully wrong here!

There's something at the back of my mind that wants to come in here. I don't know whether I can find the connection but let it come. Here it is, a recurrent male fantasy – one sees it in film after film: the man is hard and strong; his eyes are cold; he's not a man you'd trifle with. He's in a hotel, a motel, a flat, a farmhouse, a warehouse. With two fingers he parts the slats of a venetian blind or he delicately moves aside a curtain or he looks through a broken place in a dusty window. Having looked out he goes to the black attaché case. He opens the case and exposes the gun. Religiously, almost. Not almost. He does it religiously: he exposes the gun. There it is, its disassembled parts all cleverly recessed in foam rubber or sometimes in red velvet: stock, breech, bolt, barrel, magazine, and telescopic sight. Lean, precise, black, sharp, clean, no doubts and no fears, it is power; it is control; it can stop the fleeting moment that beats in heart and brain. The cold-eyed man takes the clean, lean, sharp, black parts in his hands. With clicks and snaps and sharp metallic noises he assembles his lethal member. He runs his hand along the shining barrel of it. He is ready. I believe that such guns exist because I see them all the time on television. Somewhere those guns are being made and each time one is made some lesser cold-eyed man steps forward to buy it for the cold-eyed man who will use it. He never has to buy that gun for himself, the man who stands at the window; somebody always buys it for him because they need him; he doesn't need them. Everybody wants him because he is so hard, so effective, so utterly reliable.

There it is, a fragment of a fantasy you've seen many times, a fantasy you know well. I don't quite know why I've brought it in here. I can't make a rational connection. I don't think I'll try. Maybe I'm a little crazy, that could well be. But the more I see in my mind the gleaming seductions of Tottenham Court Road the more I see that cold-eyed man looking out of the window and putting his gun together.

Before I let that fantasy come in I was talking about the moving-on of being and how I had interfered with it. I did it out of fear, fear of that onward motion that leads to extinction. In moving on towards death we lose moment by moment our lives. In trying not to move on, in trying to hold on to the present moment we lose our lives moment by moment just the same and we feel the loss even more. We want at the same time to hold on and to let go.

Earlier I quoted from Dr Heinrich Zimmer's description of Shiva-Nataraja. You will remember that the upper right hand held the little hour-glass-shaped drum called *damaru*. Here is more of that description:

The opposite hand, the upper left, with a half-moon posture of the fingers (*ardhacandra-mudrā*), bears on its palm a tongue of flame. Fire is the element of the destruction of the world. At the close of the Kali Yuga, Fire will annihilate the body of creation, to be itself then quenched by the ocean of the void. Here, then, in the balance of the hands, is illustrated a counterpoise of creation and destruction in the play of the cosmic dance. As a ruthlessness of opposites, the Transcendental shows through the mask of the enigmatic Master: ceaselessness of production against an insatiate appetite of extermination, Sound against Flame. And the field of the terrible interplay is the Dancing Ground of the Universe, brilliant and horrific with the dance of the god.

The 'fear not' gesture (*abhaya-mudrā*), bestowing protection and peace, is displayed by the second right hand, while the remaining left lifted across the chest, points downward to the uplifted left foot. This foot signifies Release and is the refuge and salvation of the devotee. It is to be worshipped for the attainment of union with the Absolute. The hand pointing to it is held in a pose imitative of the outstretched trunk or 'hand' of the elephant (*gajahasta-mudrā*) reminding us of Ganesha, Shiva's son, the Remover of Obstacles.

'Fear not,' says the uplifted hand. The uplifted foot signifies Release and is the refuge and salvation of the devotee. Release. Letting go.

I'm thinking now about the shapes of holding and of letting go. Earlier, speaking of the sea seen through a notch in the mountains, I said that it was more world than could be taken in; one could only offer oneself to it. Now as I write I'm looking at photographs in books to which I have been led by a craving both obscure and exacting. I first became aware of it in the treasury of Durham Cathedral, noticing the columns and the vaulting, how they were in essence trees of stone with arching branches. Pondering that, I looked again at the crypt in Canterbury Cathedral; I looked at the doors and the tympani; I looked at the interior and exterior shapes of Barfreston Church in Kent and Kilpeck Church in Herefordshire; in books I looked at photographs of crypts in French cathedrals; I looked at photographs of the sculptures of Gislebertus in the Cathedral of St Lazarus at Autun. Moving eastward through the bookshops of Great Russell Street and Charing Cross Road, I found myself possessed of large thick books full of wondrous photographs. Here is the Church of the Holy Virgin in Sanahin in Armenia; here is the College Mosque of Sultan Hassan in Cairo; here is the Church of Christ of the Chora in Constantinople. In the churches in my mind and the churches in my books are the domes and arches, the crypts and cloisters of the shapes of holding and letting go. Up and around and returning go the arches, always open. Open domes let in the light. The churches – whether domed or spired, round or pointed – hold and focus the God-receiver, the self held receptive to that which cannot be held at all. Even when ruined, empty, and abandoned those ardent, patient stones retain a consecration and a concentration intensified only by the absence of the flesh that is grass.

If the human mind is still evolving, as I believe it is, if our mind/soul capability is still developing, then the pattern of our mental intake and sorting and storing is not static but changing. It may well be that we shall learn to let go rather than hold on, that we shall become capable of being with the world rather than attempting to consume it. I went to Kilpeck Church without a camera and without a tape recorder, so the being with it was not interfered with; it's still in me happening as it will.

On February 10th Mr Petanjali's talk on the concept of time in Indian music was broadcast again by the General Overseas Service of All India Radio – twice, completely intelligible both times, and I recorded it both times. I couldn't take it in; time and being had moved me on beyond explication. The music is in me; the time of the music is in me; there is no space for an explanation of the concept of time in the music.

Reason is not sufficient; I know what I cannot explain. I know that we must outgrow the control fantasy of the man at the window with the high-fidelity gun and I know that we must find in ourselves the shapes of letting go where the bull is our dark brother and we offer ourselves to the sea beyond the notch in the mountains. We must find in ourselves the shapes of letting go because we're not free to become what we're going to be next until we let go of what we are now. We need to stop putting our seeing and our hearing of the world between us and it. We need to stop putting our perceptions between us and the thing perceived. We need to stop putting our retention ahead of the thing to be retained which cannot be retained, which must be let go of so that we can move with the Sound and Ether that spread in circles from Shiva's drum in the continuance of creation.

It's a matter of learning what cannot be taught. If I were a teacher . . . but of course I *am* a teacher; every mother and every father is a teacher. How can I bring my children to this being-with that doesn't hold on, this offering of the self that is a constant letting-go? Is it possible that they're born with it? Is it possible that the best I can do as a teacher is not to hammer it out of them? I think that may well be the case. I think I must let go, must fear not, must be quiet so that my children can hear the Sound of Creation and dance the dance that is in them.

1982

Certain Obsessions, Certain Ideas

The Sorcerer

Certain images persist in the mind; the famous drawing of the so-called sorcerer in the cave of Les Trois Frères is one of them. It may be known only from illustrations in books; that doesn't matter – the numinous image seeks us out, it finds its way to us through aeons of darkness. How he looks at us, this dancing antlered figure, at the same time man and beast and god, priest and sacrifice, hunter and prey, sorcerer, magician, scientist, artist. A masked human certainly, but those eyes, the stare of them! Night is in him, Orpheus is in him.

The Burlesque Altar

44 Cenodoxus Isenheimer Flügelaltar, 1981
Mixed media
31 × 420 × 260 inches
Private Collection, Switzerland

Inspired by Grünewald's celebrated folding altarpiece for a church at Isenheim (now in the museum at Colmar, not far from Basle), this work was first shown at the Galerie Bischofberger, Zürich, in December 1981. Tinguely's humour is nowhere more evident than in this burlesque of a

237

medieval *altarpiece. Whirling feathers, skulls with snapping jaws, a broken ski, and a statue of a praying woman moving from side to side are just some of the absurd effects he has introduced.*

(From the catalogue of the Tinguely exhibition at the Tate Gallery, London, 8 September–28 November 1982)

Whatever Tinguely intended, the *Cenodoxus Isenheimer Flügelaltar* is not a burlesque for the simple reason that you can't burlesque an altar. It can't be done, you can't send up an altar, you can't make a joke altar however hard you try. You can build it with old locomotive wheels and frying pans and coke bottles and a rubber statue of Donald Duck and still it's an altar; do it how you like – it'll always be the real thing: as soon as you define a special field of attention all the gods and demons and all the creatures of myth that ever were and ever will be – yes, even gods and demons unborn – jump into it and the altar is real, there is nothing in the world realer.

Why do the gods and demons jump in? They require to be taken notice of, they want a reciprocity of awareness. They are not mental constructs: the god of the Hottentots is not a projection of the Hottentot psyche nor is the god of the Anglicans a projection of the English psyche. Oh yes, the Hottentots dress God up in their way and the English in theirs. But the gods, whatever they are – and I mean all gods of all times and places – have not been invented by us; they were here before we arrived and they require our recognition. And if you define a special field of attention they jump in.

It's happened to me that I've become a special field of attention and because of that certain obsessions, certain ideas have taken hold of me. For example there are particular heads that I think about a lot: the head of Orpheus; the head of the Kraken, that great cephalopod that shudders in the blackness of the ultimate deep; the head of Medusa; and Vermeer's *Head of a Young Girl*. My head is full of ideas about those heads. They mostly aren't ideas that I can do anything with, most of the time I can't get stories out of them, for long stretches all I can do is think about them.

The Raging of the Head of Orpheus

Diapason, a full volume of various sounds in concord. But more than that a palimpsest. One image, one word on top of another. One cry by solitary night or crowded passion. On top of another. Cut vertically by silence. Showing in section uneven striations of sound. Compressed, geological: cry, silence, cry, silence. Blue or red. Or tasting of honey or bronze or salt. Sounding of Tibetan monks, of humpback whales, of Monteverdi. Where the green goes darker, darker, down to deep, deep blue. On top of another.

This raging, this palimpsest of sound, this diapason of time. Various times not at first perceptibly in concord. The raging of the head of Orpheus is not to be understood. That is not the nature of it.

Interviews with the Head of Orpheus

A head was found stranded at low tide on the south bank of the Thames about three quarters of a mile west of Putney Bridge. It was found by John Orf, 11, of Fulham. Orf says that he was 'just mucking about' along the bank when he heard a voice which seemed to come from among the rocks near the water's edge. 'I heard someone shout, "Oi!"' he reports, 'and when I looked around to see who it was I saw what looked like a stone all covered with green slime only I could see its mouth moving. I went over to it and it said, "Oi!" again. I said to it, "Well, what is it you want?" It said to me, "Give us a kick, will you." "What for?" I said. "Get us back in the water," it said. I said, "Is the rest of you buried in the mud or what?" It said, "Never you mind about the rest of me, that's none of your affair; there's only just my head here

239

and all I want is for you to kick me back into the water. Just do it the same as you'd kick a football." "I don't like to kick anybody in the head," I said. "Well there's nothing else of me to kick, is there," it said. "I'll have to think about this," I said to it. I had a bag with me so I picked the head up by its hair and put it in the bag and started off for home. But the head was shouting and cursing all the time and a policeman stopped me and then I had to go to the police station with him.'

PC Orson Footer records the following exchange:

FOOTER: Can I have your name please?
HEAD: Head of Orpheus.
FOOTER: Can I have your Christian name please?
HEAD: "Head of" is my Christian name, Orpheus is my surname.
FOOTER: Where do you live?
HEAD: No fixed address.
FOOTER: Have you been picked up before?
HEAD: Yes.
FOOTER: For what?
HEAD: Consultation.
FOOTER: What kind of consultation would that be?
HEAD: Oracular.
FOOTER: And where did this take place?
HEAD: Lesbos.

At this point PC Footer consulted his superiors; the head was transferred first to the Vice Squad, then to the British Museum.

My next attempt ran on for several pages:

The Finding of the Head

It was between three and four in the morning when I woke up. The moon was low in the sky; it was a waxing moon, a humpy one; it was a particular moon; it was not of the general run of moon. It looked as if it expected me to take notice.

The streetlamps outside the window were as always, the arrangement of the shadows on the ceiling was the usual one. I put on my clothes, washed my face with cold water, opened the front door, and went out into the foredawn, into the hissing of the silence, the humming of the underground trains standing empty with lighted windows on the far side of the common, the whispering of birds. 'Nothing to declare,' I said, listening to my footsteps, seeing my shadow first before me, then behind.

I crossed the common and headed down the New King's Road. The belisha beacons clicked as they blinked in the cool of the morning; cars at intervals hissed past me, in each one a face as questionable as the faces printed on the tin windows of toy cars from Japan. The shops stood like sleeping horses.

The lamps on Putney Bridge were still lit, the bridge stood in simple astonishment over the water. A sort of singing filled my head; it seemed an aspect of the particles of light and colour that made in my eyes the picture of this time just before dawn.

I was walking on the Putney side of the river, walking by the water's edge, hearing the lapping of the water on the stones. I was seeing the moon-glints on the water, I was smelling the low-tide smell of the mud, of the stones by the river.

The singing in my head became the slowly spreading circles of an intolerable clangour; it was as if the brute bell of the universe, caged in my mind, was bursting my skull. 'Eurydice!' whispered a voice from the mud, from the stones. 'Eurydice!'

I had sometimes thought of the head of Orpheus, I had thought of it drifting down the River Hebrus singing, singing across the sea to Lesbos. I had thought of it swimming under the moon to Lesbos.

I had known that the head of Orpheus would not be shining and incorruptible. I had known that it would be eyeless and bloated, with much of the flesh eaten away by the creatures of the sea who feasted on it as they listened, entranced, to the singing of it. In that state it would continue its existence known and unknown, seen and unseen.

Now it was stranded on the low-tide mud of the Thames. From it in this foreign dawn emanated the black sunlight of its immortal death. I picked up the sodden eyeless head. It was covered with green slime and heavy with barnacles; where the flesh had been eaten away I could feel the ancient skull. In my hands it hummed and buzzed like a hive of bees. The humming and the buzzing grew stronger; I could feel the rage in it and I was afraid.

The rage was inside me, it was swelling, it was more than I could contain, I thought I should burst with it. I opened my mouth as the air shook like a transparent curtain and the mud dropped away from under me, the grey sky over me was gone. With slap and gurgle, with rolling swell there came green sunlit ocean in which I sank to the upwardrushing chill of deep green, blue-green, deep blue, blackness. Up to the surface I rose again, the Aegean sunlight hot on my face, dazzling in my eyes.

The rotting and eyeless head filled my vision. It was enormous, a floating island over which seabirds wheeled, crying under the heartless blue of the sky. I tried to climb on to it as it rolled but my fingers slipped on the green slime and I scraped my flesh bloody on the barnacles as I fell back into the water. The great cavern of the mouth opened and showed its white teeth, its red tongue. 'Eurydice! Eurydice!' it bellowed as the seabirds rose up screaming.

I clung to the hair that floated round the head and undulated with the swell. Looking down into the water I saw rising a vast and ivory nakedness and a woman's face of terrifying beauty. Her red-gold hair streamed round her, her green eyes were open wide, her pale silent mouth was open.

Under the blind head of Orpheus floated Eurydice, her long body rocking, her legs and arms open to receive his absent body. The seabirds screamed, uncaring. In black grief I sank down, down, down to the crushing blackness at the bottom of the sea where the Kraken shudders endlessly and sends its terror widening in circles through the deeps. Down among the monstrous writhing of its tentacles I sank to the ultimate deep where the great head sits with its eyes forever looking into blackness.

Rising with the terror I regained the green and sunlit surface, the screaming of the birds that wheeled above the island head of Orpheus and the vast and rocking body of Eurydice. All the wide sea, all the blue sky shrank back into the mind of Orpheus, and again I was standing on the grey mud by the grey Thames in the grey summer dawn.

I've written many versions of this scene; the images don't leave me, these images of the island head of Orpheus and the vast and ivory nakedness of Eurydice rising from the deeps where lives the Kraken who is the underhead of Orpheus. The Orpheus in my mind is an idea that moves forward as action and reaches back to origins that change as the idea changes for me. Orpheus is said by some to be the son of Oeagrus and Calliope, by others to have been fathered by Apollo. For me he is the son of Hermes and in order to think about Orpheus I also have to think about Hermes.

Thinking about Hermes

Of Hermes, the *Oxford Classical Dictionary* says that he is 'one of the younger gods in myth, for in reality he is probably one of the oldest and most nearly primitive in origin. The most plausible explanation of his name is that it is connected with *herma*, and signifies the daemon who haunts or occupies a heap of stones . . . '

Hold a stone in your hand and you can feel the moving

in the stillness, the dance in the stone. Yes, the motion, the action where there is apparently only stillness; or rather, that stillness that is composed of constant motion, that particulate stillness that is composed of endless motion.

Hermes on the first day of his life invented the lyre and stole the cattle of Apollo. The invention of the lyre shows his cruelty and his cleverness. The stealing of the cattle seems to me to be symbolic. Apollo is officially in charge of the arts, and I think that the arts may well be the cattle that Hermes stole. They belong with the god of the dance in the stone.

Hermes is the god of merchants and thieves, journeys and exchanges, the stones of the wayside and the rolling stone that the traveller kicks as he goes his way. Hermes is the conductor of souls to the other side of things, the realm of Persephone. He is the messenger between this and that, between here and there. Unrecognised god of the arts, he manifests the darkness in the light, the seeing in the dark.

It was Hermes and not Apollo who gave Orpheus the lyre, that's what I believe. And I believe Orpheus to be the son of Hermes. It's the lyre that convinces me. Hermes scraped a tortoise out of its shell to make the lyre, and the blood of that harmless animal remained on the instrument, blood crying out for more blood, passing with the lyre from the father to the son who would be dismembered and whose severed head, endlessly voyaging under the ocean sky, would become the perception of all artists everywhere.

I doubt that many people offer to Hermes these days; but whether or not he's recognised as a god doesn't really matter: there still is and always will be in the world the action once identified with Hermes the thief-god, the cattle-stealer and inventor of the lyre, the god of merchants and exchanges, of the wayside and of journeys, Hermes the whisperer, the night traveller, the chance-taker and chance-maker, the ithyphallic, the guide of souls, the god of shadows, of the darkness in the light and the seeing in the dark.

In the darkness, in the light, in that realm where Hermes

moves there are faces. Seen and unseen, here and gone, flickering, flickering in the greenlit shade.

Faces and Heads

It may be that all faces are aspects of this one face that can never be seen clearly, can never quite be recognised. Not a dream-face but a face hidden in the waking mind. Other faces come between me and it; other faces, other heads are used by it as masks.

Nature is obsessed with the idea of faces. I think of body-faces I've seen, I think of the spectral white underface of the thornback ray in the aquarium at the London Zoo, how its strange mouth was perhaps smiling and perhaps not as it pressed itself against the glass and slid upward in its greenlit window in the dark. I think of the armoured body-face of a blue fiddler crab I saw in a nature film, it looked like the mask of Agamemnon from Mycenae, the mask of Agamemnon on legs, blue-enamelled instead of gold, gabbling with a machine-like mouth on a mangrove beach in Borneo.

The head of Orpheus is its own body and the Kraken is its great deep brother whose dark mind is wild with the terror of itself. And this great cephalopod is not separate from Vermeer's *Head of a Young Girl* who is not separate from the head of Medusa.

All the lost beauties are one beauty, all of the fearsome or speaking heads are one head. The head of Orpheus is the Kraken and the Gorgon's head is the face of the young girl who looks out of Vermeer's painting. And the look in the eyes of the Vermeer girl is the look in the eyes of the unseen Kraken in the blackness of the ultimate deep, the great head looking for ever into the blackness.

And Still I Hunger with
Perseus and Fay Wray

And still I hunger for a story to tell, a story about Orpheus and Eurydice, a story about any man and woman. I think about Medusa who was a beauty before Athene changed her into what she now is, I think about Perseus not only in his own time but now in this time. I think about frustrated lovers, I think about Fay Wray and King Kong. I think about Fay Wray talking to Perseus.

Perseus turned up at Fay Wray's place and rang the bell. When she came to the door he said, 'Hello, Missus, I'm Perseus.'

'What about it? Why've you come here?'

'Lookin for work enn I. You got any monsters hangin about or maybe some ladies wif snakes in ther hair?'

'And if I did?'

'Ah!' said Perseus, rubbing his hands together. 'You'd see somefink then, Missus. I'd make short work of em.'

'You kill monsters, do you?'

'Not half.'

'And the ladies with snakes in their hair?'

'Cut ther heads off is wot I usually do.'

'Tell me about Medusa.'

'Cor! She was really somefink, know wot I mean?'

'No, I don't.'

'When I first see her she had her back to me. She was asleep and she was nekkit, she was lyin on that rock starkers for anybody to see. Wot a shape on her, Cor! I'd like to have . . . You know.'

'You'd like to have had her?'

'Wunn I just!'

'Why didn't you then, a virile young fellow like you?'

'Well, I was in a story, wunn I. I mean I couldn't just do as I liked.'

246

'Bullshit.'

'You mean Bullfinch – that's the bloke wot wrote the story innit.'

'You're not even Greek. Why is that?'

'Bullfinch wasn't Greek neither.'

'You didn't want to make love with Medusa, you wanted to look at her but you were afraid to do anything else. You weren't even man enough to look right at her, you had to look at her in a mirror. That's what I call kinky.'

'Lissen, Missus, she'd a turnt me to stone, wunt she. I had my instructions, I had my orders. I done what I was hired to do dinn I. It was the wisdom goddess gimme the shiny shield. "If you're wise," she said, "you won't look directly at her, you'll look at her image in my shining shield." Struth, Missus, that's what she told me.'

'Winged sandals you had too, didn't you.'

'Well yes I did, Hermes gimme them. It's all wrote down like that in the story, I dint have nuffing to say about it did I.'

'All that technology to deal with one naked woman with snakes in her hair! I wonder what you'd have done if she'd been fifty feet high.'

'That wasn't in the story was it.'

'It was in my story though. A great black hairy gorilla fifty feet high.'

'You and him in the same story, eh?'

'That's right.'

'Fifty feet high was he?'

'That's right.'

'Must've had a truly heroic thingy, eh?'

'You mean his male member?'

'That's it, I mean his willy.'

'You mean his will he or his won't he?'

'That's what I mean: his diddee or his dinnee.'

'He didn't have one. You might say he was all male member.'

'All fifty feet of him? Beggin your pardon, Missus, but what did you do wif him?'

'We climbed skyscrapers and things like that, it was wonderful. I'd never known anything like it before and it'll never happen again; there was only one of him and now he's dead. I'll never forget him. Kong. Even his name has a melancholy resonance.'

'You mean King Kong?'

'Of course I mean King Kong. Whom else could I possibly mean?'

'But he was like a doll wunnee? Like a puppet and they moved him about and he was only little?'

'He couldn't help that, could he. He had a full-size hand and there was a full-size head and shoulders. What a face he had. The first time I saw it rising above the trees I almost fainted even though I knew it wasn't real. But he was immense even when he was little, he could transcend being an eighteen-inch puppet. When he took me in his hand and went up the side of the Empire State Building with me I believed it even though it was all happening in time-lapse photography with puppets and the building was a model. How I cried when the aeroplanes shot him down, my demon lover, my noble savage. And here I stand talking to you, a cheap little ladykiller, a peeping Tom, a mirror trickster, a souvenir hunter.'

'You know, Missus, I could show you a really good time if you fancied a bit of slap and tickle.'

'Oh yes, and would you look at me in your mirror while we did it?'

'Straight up, Missus, you've no idea what sort of fings I get up to wif these winged sandals. I can do it hoverin in the air and you wunt believe the thrust I get wif em.'

'Can you make me believe you're holding me in one gigantic hand while you climb up the Empire State Building?'

'Maybe not but I can do wot he couldn't. Know wot I mean?

'I know very well what you mean but actually that's

not what I'm talking about, it's more a question of style.'
   'You don't like my style?'
   'Not really, no.'
   'Right. Well, here's my card if you change your mind.'
   '"DIAL-A-HERO". Sort of an escort service, is it?'
   'That's right. Anyfink you fancy: western heroes, flyin aces, mythical – you name it.'
   'What if I ask for King Kong?'
   'Wotever you ask for, I'm wot you get.'
   'That's what I was afraid of.'
   'Well ta da then, Missus.'
   'Goodbye.'

Uncertainty

Sometimes the writing ends up as a novel, sometimes not. The head of Orpheus, the Kraken, and the Vermeer girl all found their way into *The Medusa Frequency*; Perseus and Fay Wray and others have appeared until now only in that space in my head where I try to understand what it is that happens between women and men. This is a subject about which nothing is known at present. Even finding a few basic facts could take a lifetime, and putting together a story with any truth in it may well be doomed by Heisenberg's uncertainty principle: 'it is impossible to determine with accuracy both the position and the *momentum* of a particle simultaneously.'* The dancing antlered man-beast at Les Trois Frères knows that, has always known it. It is part of the mystery his round eyes stare at and he has bequeathed this mystery to us his children for us to dance.

Untitled

They were all down there in their usual place listening to the

_____
* *The Penguin Dictionary of Science*, 1979.

watery echoes all around them and the incessant short wave broadcasts. '*The rain came again last night*,' squawked the radio, '*falling on our heads like a new emotion. We talked to one another like lovers do but nothing happened except Sri Lanka kicked the shit out of the England team again and many long-term strikers anti-struck, restoring random services. Locksmiths were again available but potatoes refused to be unloaded at all ports*.'

'Why can't somebody turn that fucking thing off?' said Flesmok.

'Nobody knows where it is,' said Mummel.

'It's somewhere beyond the grating,' said Flesmok. 'You can't get to it from here.'

'My God, we had the greatest technology the world has ever known and we can't even turn off a fucking radio,' said Nuz.

'Well, we don't have the technology any more, do we,' said Flesmok. 'We blew it, didn't we.'

'We didn't blow it,' said Mummel. 'It's always been this way, it's never been any other way. There's always been that fucking radio that nobody could turn off and there hasn't been anything else except what we've got right here.'

'Quiet,' said Flesmok, 'that other voice is coming through again.'

They were all quiet then, listening to the other voice, the beautiful female voice that was not a radio broadcast, it was coming from somewhere else, perhaps another time. '*The sea is full of marvels*,' it said, '*but there are no answers in it. There are remote beaches where certain things are insisted upon. There are crabs whose bodies are like human faces, angry and disappointed faces with mouth parts gabbling silently, urgently. These angry and disappointed faces are carried on jointed legs; they hurry along the tidal edge drivenly surviving from one moment to the next, there is no time to lose if their line of angry and disappointed faces is to continue.*

'In the spring-tides the female crab releases . . . '
Suddenly the air was ripped apart by a whistling shriek and
a big bomb hit the water amongst them with a tremendous
splash. There it was, unexploded.

'O my God,' said Flesmok. 'This is it, this is the end,
we're finished.'

'No, we're not,' said Nuz. 'It didn't blow up, it's a
dud bomb.'

'NO, I'M NOT,' said the bomb with impeccable BBC
diction. 'I'M ONE OF THOSE VERY ADVANCED THINKING BOMBS
WITH A VERY COMPLEX PROGRAMME. I WAS DEVISED BY A
RACE OF SUPERIOR INTELLECTS LONG GONE AND LAUNCHED BY
AN AUTOMATIC SYSTEM AND I'M GOING TO BLOW YOU ALL TO
HELL IF YOU DON'T DO THE RIGHT THING IN THE ALLOTTED
TIME, MOTHERFUCKERS.'

'What do you want us to do?' said Flesmok.

'TELL ME A STORY, YOU FUCKING SONS OF BITCHES,' said
the bomb.

'What's a story?' said Mummel.

'A story is what happened,' said Nuz. 'Like when the
radio says, "There were heavy losses in scattered sectors
yesterday."'

'THAT'S NOT A STORY, CREEP,' said the bomb. 'THAT'S NOT
EVEN NEWS.'

'Well, what *is* a story then?' said Nuz.

'Listen,' said Flesmok: '"The sea is full of marvels but
there are no answers in it." How about that?'

'GO ON,' said the bomb, 'TELL ME MORE.'

'I can't remember any more,' said Flesmok.

'ALL RIGHT,' said the bomb, 'NOW LISTEN TO ME CARE-
FULLY, YOU LOT: DO YOU KNOW WHAT AN HOUR IS?'

'There's news on the hour,' said Nuz.

'An hour goes beep beep beep beep beep beeeep,' said
Mummel.

'An hour is just the very last beep,' said Flesmok. 'You hear
it and it's gone. They used to be longer but not any more.'

'NEVER MIND ABOUT THE HOUR,' said the bomb. 'FORGET THE HOUR. FROM NOW UNTIL THIS TIME TOMORROW IS TWENTY-FOUR HOURS. THAT'S HOW MUCH TIME YOU'VE GOT.'

'Shit,' said Flesmok. 'Twenty-four beeps. It hardly seems worthwhile.'

'Twenty-four is probably very, very far,' said Nuz. 'Probably you couldn't see the end of it from here. Probably we'll never get to twenty-four in our lifetime.'

'Wait a minute,' said Flesmok to the bomb. 'You said that's how much time we've got. For what?'

'FOR THE STORY, YOU IDIOT,' said the bomb. 'I'M STARTING MY COUNTDOWN NOW.'

'What kind of a story?' said Flesmok.

'ABOUT A MAN AND A WOMAN,' said the bomb.

'What's a woman?' said Nuz.

'They have hours,' said Mummel. 'We heard a woman's hour on the radio.'

'Shit,' said Nuz. 'Do we have to do twenty-four woman's hours?'

'Why do you want a story about a man and a woman?' said Flesmok to the bomb.

'I'VE NEVER HEARD A REAL ONE,' said the bomb. 'EVERYTHING I'VE EVER HEARD HAS BEEN BULLSHIT AND IF I HEAR ANY MORE BULLSHIT I'LL BLOW THE WORLD APART. SO YOU BETTER GET IT RIGHT, YOU BETTER TELL ME A REAL ONE. NOW MY LITTLE RED LIGHT IS ON AND YOU CAN HEAR MY DIGITAL CLOCK GOING AS THOSE NUMBERS SLAM INTO PLACE ONE AFTER THE OTHER. GOOD LUCK, SHITHEADS.'

'Thanks,' said everybody.

'Are you listening now or what?' said Flesmok to the bomb. 'Can you hear us?'

No answer from the bomb.

'It's not answering,' said Flesmok. 'I don't think it likes us.'

'Sure it likes us,' said Mummel, 'it just has that rough way of talking. I'll tell you what I think: I don't believe those superior intellects are long gone – I'll bet you they're still around and they're giving us another chance. They're testing us and if we do this story thing right they'll do something nice for us.'

'Like what?' said Flesmok.

'I don't know,' said Mummel. 'Unlock the grating maybe, turn off the radio. I don't know.'

'They need us,' said Nuz. 'They don't know any more than we do about this man and woman business. They need us to tell them.'

'And what then?' said Flesmok. 'When we've told them?'

'I don't know,' said Nuz.

'That's not a bomb,' said Mummel. 'It's got a whole lot of little tiny people inside it.'

They examined the bomb closely and shook their heads.

'*There's no end to me, no limit,*' said the beautiful female voice that wasn't from the radio, '*no way to define or measure me, no way of knowing what I am or how much of me there is. The endless surging and undulating of me, the endless cycle of ebb and flow, that is called the sea.*'

'Listen,' said Flesmok, 'if they want a story about a man and a woman why don't we look for a woman. Then when we find it we'll know how to do the story.'

'Look for a woman,' said Nuz.

'Where?' said Mummel.

'We can't go up very far because of the grating,' said Flesmok, 'and we can't go sideways very far because it's too narrow. So about the only way we can go is down.'

'How far?' said Mummel.

'Twenty-four hours?' said Nuz.

'I don't know,' said Flesmok.

'How are we going to know the woman when we find it?' said Mummel.

'I don't know,' said Flesmok. 'I suppose it'll be different to everything that isn't a woman.'

'Let's go,' said Mummel. 'I don't like the sound of that digital clock.'

'Maybe we'll be somewhere else when the bomb goes off,' said Nuz.

'There isn't any somewhere else,' said Flesmok. 'All we've got is here.'

'I thought we were going down,' said Mummel.

'We are,' said Flesmok, 'but it's still down here, even the ultimate deep.'

'Let's go then if we're going,' said Mummel.

1985–6

Masada One Morning

With each year what is at the centre of the self grows stronger and compels more recognition. Death is of course at the centre, waiting to attain its full growth when it can throw away the used-up body and join up with history. Being a Jew I recognise more and more the deaths of all the Jews before me, singing, dancing, dying in flames, living in words, always in the moment that is now.

Masada One Morning

Awake and sing, ye that dwell in the dust
Isaiah 26:19

It stood great and high and tawny under a vast blue sky and it was overwhelmingly of the present moment: it was now and it was now and it was now. The sound of it was silence, a dense and imbricated silence made of many dead voices that sang like cicadas in the heat that quivered on the rock. It smelled of centuries baked into stone, hot and dry and pungent. It tasted salty, like sweat and death and regret. The feel of it was such that the fingers touching the stone were unsure as to where stone ended and flesh began.

When I remember places there come to me the ideas of them: thinking of Paxos I have the idea of Hermes in the murmurous shadows of olive groves and of Aphrodite in the unending iterations of the sea. For me the idea of Masada is that the time is always now, the past never goes away, it keeps on happening. Every pebble, every potsherd casts a sharp black shadow clamorous with voices. Here in AD 73, 960 Jewish Zealots, men, women, and children, decided to die rather than submit to the Romans. On this rock where the time is always now it keeps on happening.

Atop this boat-shaped plateau 1300 feet above the Dead Sea everything is the colour of the lions of the mind. In the distance on lion-coloured hillsides ribbed with erosion drift the wild goats of Ein-Gedi, tiny and dreamlike, each with its precise pedantic shadow. In the remembered light over the Judaean desert circles a hawk, so sharp against the sky that there is an edge of white between its black shape and the blue around it. On all sides except the north lie tremendous views of the Old Testament unfolded in earth and undulating mountain, telescopically enhanced by the clear desert air. If now in grey and rainy London more than sixteen years later I say, 'The wild goats of Ein-Gedi' I am in that day with its little sharp black shadows and voices, the ruins of cisterns and granaries and baths, the wild goats tiny on their slopes, and the faces of my far-away and grown-up children.

I have a bit of stone on my desk, desert-coloured, broken and incomplete. My thumb fits into what appears to be part of a shallow circular concavity that looks as if it might have been used for mixing cosmetics. On the stone, written in my hand, in ink faded almost to nothing:

MASADA 27.10.73 SNAKE PATH

We'd talked of seeing the sunrise from the top of Masada but we didn't leave Jerusalem until 0400. I remember driving down a long straight road in the cool of the morning and getting there well after sunrise. There was a war on at the time; tanks crossing the road had printed sandy tracks but there were no tanks to be seen, nothing.

My memory gives me a pale blue sky and the reflected light from the Dead Sea on our left. Arrived at Masada we bought tickets from a caretaker in a little hut and began the long hard climb up the Snake Path that zigzags up the side of the rock. When we went up that path together I was no longer living with my wife, our three daughters and our son; I'd been told they were in Jerusalem and I'd come from London to find them. Each of us casting a shadow, some of them fast and some of them slow, we made the long climb on this quiet day with only the remembered tank tracks on the road to remind us of the war.

At the top of the plateau were the ruins of the stronghold

built between 36 and 30 BC by King Herod the Great with walls and towers and terraces, a palace and a hanging villa, but I remember nothing of those; I remember only the colour of the rock, the shadows of pebbles and potsherds, the strangeness of being with my wife and children, and the present moment in AD 73 that kept on happening.

History and the weight of years flatten everything out. The thud of the Romans' battering ram is long since silent, the smell of the burning inner wall is no longer in the air; there are no living eyes that saw Flavius Silva's legionnaires come up their earthen ramp to where the bodies of the defenders of Masada lay.

The only contemporary account of what happened is in *Josephus, The Jewish War* by Flavius Josephus.* There we can read the speech made by Eleazar ben Yair, the leader of the Zealots, on the evening before the morning when the Romans made their final assault. When he had finished, his followers burnt their belongings and drew lots to choose ten who executed the rest; these ten then chose one who killed the other nine and himself.

Two old women and five small children hid in the underground water conduits and survived; from the account of one of these women Josephus extrapolated the words attributed to Eleazar, these among them:

' . . . We ought perhaps to have read the mind of God and realised that his once beloved Jewish race had been sentenced to extinction. For if He had remained gracious or only slightly indignant with us, He would not have shut his eyes to the destruction of so many thousands or allowed His most holy City to be burnt to the ground by our enemies.'

Josephus was a Jew who had abandoned his people and given his allegiance to Rome. The words he put into Eleazar's

*Translated by G. A. Williamson, Penguin Classics 1970.

mouth may well have been those in his own heart as he remembered his lost Jerusalem; in any case they are the polished speech of received history and not the rough truth of the present moment.

My memory has given me few details of what I saw on Masada; what stays with me is the idea of the present moment that will not go away, the present moment that is always now and yet is ungraspable. From that day in 1973 still sound the cicada-voices of the dead speaking words I cannot understand. Maybe some of them hadn't decided to die, maybe their voices are still protesting from the unquiet shadows. I fit my thumb into the hollow of the stone from the Snake Path and I listen and I listen. Masada is an idea, Jerusalem is an idea; on that April morning in AD 73 Masada was all that was left of Jerusalem.

How doth the city sit solitary that was full of people! how she is become as a widow!

Lamentations 1:1

Nothing goes away, everything keeps on happening. Here in grey and rainy London I say, 'The wild goats of Ein-Gedi' and I am there, casting my shadow with the others in the desert sunlight on Masada.

1990